Between Parent and Child

Between Parent and Child

The Bestselling Classic
That Revolutionized
Parent-Child Communication

DR. HAIM G. GINOTT

Revised and Updated by

DR. ALICE GINOTT & DR. H. WALLACE GODDARD

 THREE RIVERS PRESS
NEW YORK

Published by Three Rivers Press, New York, New York.
Member of the Crown Publishing Group, a division of Random House, Inc.
www.randomhouse.com

THREE RIVERS PRESS and the Tugboat design are registered trademarks of
Random House, Inc.

Originally published in hardcover by Macmillan in 1965.

Printed in the United States of America

Design by Meryl Sussman Levari/Digitext

Library of Congress Cataloging-in-Publication Data
Ginott, Haim G.
    Between parent and child : the bestselling classic that revolutionized
parent-child communication / Haim G. Ginott.—Rev. and updated / by
Alice Ginott and H. Wallace Goddard.
    Includes index.
    1. Child rearing. 2. Parent and child. 3. Emotions in children.
4. Empathy. 5. Domestic education. I. Ginott, Alice. II. Goddard,
H. Wallace. III. Title.
HQ769 .G55 2003
649'.1—dc21   2003000626

ISBN 0-609-80988-1

20 19 18 17 16 15 14

Revised Edition

To the memory of my younger brother who died at the age of twenty-one, trying to save his besieged comrades.

Acknowledgments

We are grateful to friends and colleagues who read the manuscript and contributed suggestions and criticism. Special thanks to Gerald Gross, for reading some of the manuscript and for his helpful suggestions; to Claudia Gabel, our editor, whose patience and helpful suggestions have made the publishing process so much easier and more pleasant; to Betsy Rapoport, who saw the benefit of reissuing this book; to Theodore Cohn, for his patience, his help, and his valuable editorial comments; to our children and their children, who helped us appreciate the importance of caring communication; to Nancy Goddard, who has been a model of compassionate parenting; to Emily, Andy, and Sara, who have taught us priceless lessons. And, most of all, to the parents who shared with us their feelings and experience, we acknowledge our greatest debt.

HAIM G. GINOTT
ALICE GINOTT
H. WALLACE GODDARD

Contents

Preface

After my death, eulogize me thus
There was a man and he is no more
He died before his time
The song of his life was in the middle interrupted
One more song he had
And now that song is lost forever
The sorrow of it

—AFTER MY DEATH,
BY HAIM NACHMAN BIALIK

Dr. Haim Ginott died on November 4, 1973, after a long and painful illness. He was fifty-one years old. A few weeks before he died he looked at the first book he wrote, *Between Parent and Child*, and said to me, "Alice, you'll see, this book will be a classic." His prediction has come true.

Haim Ginott was a clinical psychologist, child therapist, and parent educator whose books—*Group Psychotherapy with Children, Between Parent and Child, Between Parent and Teenager,* and *Teacher and Child*—revolutionized the way parents and teachers relate to children. The books were bestsellers for more than a year and were translated into thirty languages. In *The Authoritative Guide to Self-Help Books* by John W. Santrock, Ann M. Minnett, and Barbara D. Campbell, Ginott's books received the highest rating ("strongly recommended") and appeared on the short list of best self-help books.

He was the first resident psychologist on the *Today* show; wrote a weekly column, syndicated internationally by King Features; and wrote a monthly column for *McCall's* magazine. He also served as adjunct professor of psychology at the Graduate School of New York University and the postdoctoral program at Adelphi University.

The communication skills that he advocates in his books help adults enter into the world of children in a compassionate and caring way and teach them how to become aware of and respond to feelings.

As he said in one of his speeches, "I'm a child psychotherapist. I treat disturbed children. Suppose I see children in therapy one hour a week for a year. Their symptoms disappear, they feel better about themselves, they get along with others, they even stop fidgeting in school. What is it that I do that helps? I communicate with them in a caring way. I use every opportunity to help them develop self-confidence. *If caring communication can drive sick children sane, its principles and practices belong to parents and teachers.* While psychotherapists may be able to cure, only those in daily contact with children can help them to become psychologically healthy."

Thus he started parent-education and guidance groups to help parents learn how to be more caring and effective with their children, to become aware of their own feelings, and become more understanding of their children's feelings. He wanted them to learn how to discipline without humiliating, how to criticize without demeaning, how to praise without judging, how to express anger without hurting, how to acknowledge rather than argue with their feelings, perceptions, and opinions. How to respond so that children would learn to trust their inner reality and develop self-confidence.

Before he became a psychologist, Dr. Haim Ginott was a schoolteacher in Israel. He was a graduate of David Yellin Teachers' College in Jerusalem. After teaching for a few years he realized that he was not sufficiently prepared to deal with children in the classroom. It was then that he decided to come to Columbia University Teachers College, where he received his doctorate.

Even though Haim Ginott died at a young age, he enjoyed a creative and accomplished intellectual life. His innovative ideas of communicating with children that he disseminated in his books, lectures, and columns reverberated not only in the United States but all over the world. He influenced the development of parenting workshops where parents and teachers learn how to treat children in a sensitive and caring way.

Although English was not Haim Ginott's native tongue, he loved the English language. He loved it as a poet, using it sparingly and with precision. Like the early sages he dispensed his wisdom in parables, allegories, and epigrams: "Don't be a parent, be a human being who is a parent."

A story is told about a rabbi who died at the age of fifty. When the family returned from the funeral, the eldest son said, "Our father had a long life." Everyone was aghast. "How can you say that of a man who died so young?" they asked. "Because his life was full; he wrote many important books, and touched many lives."

That is my consolation.

ALICE GINOTT, PH.D.
2003

CHILD, GIVE ME YOUR HAND
THAT I MAY WALK IN THE LIGHT
OF YOUR FAITH IN ME

—Hannah Kahn

Between
Parent and
Child

Introduction

No parent wakes up in the morning planning to make a child's life miserable. No mother or father says, "Today I'll yell, nag, and humiliate my child whenever possible." On the contrary, in the morning many parents resolve, "This is going to be a peaceful day. No yelling, no arguing, and no fighting." Yet, in spite of good intentions, the unwanted war breaks out again.

Parenthood is an endless series of small events, periodic conflicts, and sudden crises that call for a response. The response is not without consequence: It affects personality and self-regard for better or worse.

We would like to believe that only a disturbed parent responds in a way that is damaging to a child. Unfortunately, even parents who are loving and well meaning also blame, shame, accuse, ridicule, threaten, bribe, label, punish, preach, and moralize.

Why? Because most parents are unaware of the destructive power of words. They find themselves saying things that they heard their parents say to them, things they don't intend in a tone they don't like. The tragedy of such communication often lies not in the lack of caring but in a lack of understanding; not in a lack of intelligence, but in a lack of knowledge.

Parents need a special way of relating and talking with their children. How would any of us feel if a surgeon came into the operating room and before the anesthesiologist put us under, said, "I really don't have much training in surgery but I love my patients and I use common sense"? We would probably panic and run for our lives. But it's not that easy for children whose parents believe that love and common sense are enough. Like surgeons, parents, too, need to learn special skills to become competent in coping with the daily demands of children. Like a trained surgeon who is careful where he cuts, parents, too, need to become skilled in the use of words. Because words are like knives. They can inflict, if not physical, many painful emotional wounds.

Where do we start if we are to improve communication with children? By examining how we respond. We even know the words. We heard our parents use them with guests and strangers. *It is a language that is protective of feelings, not critical of behavior.*

What do we say to a guest who forgets her umbrella? Do we run after her and say, "What is the matter with you? Every time you come to visit you forget something. If it's not one thing it's another. Why can't you be like your younger sister? When she comes to visit, she knows how to behave. You're forty-four years old! Will you never learn? I'm not a slave to pick up after you! I bet you'd forget your head if it weren't attached to your shoulders!" That's not what we say to a guest. We say, "Here's your umbrella, Alice," without adding, "scatterbrain."

Parents need to learn to respond to their children as they do to guests.

Parents want their children to be secure and happy. No parent deliberately tries to make a child fearful, shy, inconsiderate, or obnoxious. Yet in the process of growing up, many children acquire undesirable characteristics and fail to achieve a sense of security and an attitude of respect for themselves and others. Parents want their children to be polite, and they are rude; they want them to be neat, and they are messy; they want them to be self-confident, and they are insecure; they want them to be happy, and often they are not.

Parents can help each child become a mensch, a human being with compassion, commitment, and courage; a person whose life is guided by a core of strength and a code of fairness. To achieve these humane goals, parents need to learn humane methods. Love is not enough. Insight is insufficient. Good parents need skill. How to attain and use such skill is the main theme of this book. It will help parents translate desired ideals into daily practices.

Hopefully, this book will also help parents identify their goals in relation to children and to suggest methods of achieving those goals. Parents are confronted with concrete problems that require specific solutions; they are not helped by cliché advice such as "Give the child more love," "Show her more attention," and "Offer him more time."

For many years, we have worked with parents and children in individual as well as in group psychotherapy and in parenting workshops. This book is the fruit of that

experience. It is a practical guide; it offers concrete suggestions and preferred solutions for dealing with daily
situations and psychological problems faced by all parents.
*It gives specific advice derived from basic communication
principles that will guide parents in living with children in
mutual respect and dignity.*

CHAPTER 1

The Code of Communication:

Parent-Child Conversations

Children's Questions: The Hidden Meanings

Conversing with children is a unique art with rules and meanings of its own. Children are rarely naive in their communications. Their messages are often in a code that requires deciphering.

Andy, age ten, asked his father, "What is the number of abandoned children in Harlem?" Andy's father, a lawyer, was glad to see his son take an interest in social problems. He gave a long lecture on the subject and then looked up the figure. But Andy was not satisfied and kept on asking questions on the same subject: "What is the number of abandoned children in New York City? In the United States? In Europe? In the world?"

Finally it occurred to Andy's father that his son was concerned not about a social problem, but about a personal one. Andy's questions stemmed not so much from sympathy for abandoned children as from fear of being abandoned. He was looking not for a figure representing the number of deserted children, but for reassurance that he would not be deserted.

Thus, his father, reflecting Andy's concern, answered, "You're worried that your parents may someday abandon you the way some parents do. Let me reassure you that we will not desert you. And should it ever bother you again, please tell me so that I can help you stop worrying."

On her first visit to kindergarten, while her mother was still with her, Nancy, age five, looked over the paintings on the wall and asked loudly, "Who made these ugly pictures?" Nancy's mother was embarrassed. She looked at her daughter disapprovingly, and hastened to tell her, "It's not nice to call the pictures ugly when they are so pretty."

The teacher, who understood the meaning of the question, smiled and said, "In here you don't have to paint pretty pictures. You can paint mean pictures if you feel like it." A big smile appeared on Nancy's face, for now she had the answer to her hidden question, "What happens to a girl who doesn't paint so well?"

Next Nancy picked up a broken fire engine and asked self-righteously, "Who broke this fire engine?" Her mother answered, "What difference does it make to you who broke it? You don't know anyone here."

Nancy was not really interested in names. She wanted to find out what happened to children who break toys. Understanding the question, the teacher gave an appropriate answer: "Toys are for playing. Sometimes they get broken. It happens."

Nancy seemed satisfied. Her interviewing skill had netted her the necessary information: This grown-up is pretty nice, she does not get angry quickly, even when a picture comes out ugly or a toy is broken, I don't have to be afraid, it is safe to stay here. Nancy waved good-bye to her mother and went over to the teacher to start her first day in kindergarten.

Carol, age twelve, was tense and tearful. Her favorite cousin was going home after staying with her during the summer. Unfortunately, her mother's response to Carol's sadness was neither empathic nor understanding.

CAROL (*with tears in her eyes*): Susie is going away. I'll be all alone again.

MOTHER: You'll find another friend.

CAROL: I'll be so lonely.

MOTHER: You'll get over it.

CAROL: Oh, Mother! (*Sobs.*)

MOTHER: You're twelve years old and still such a crybaby.

Carol gave her mother a deadly look and escaped to her room, closing the door behind her. This episode should have had a happier ending. A child's feelings must be taken seriously, even though the situation itself is not very serious. In her mother's eyes a separation at summer's end may be too minor a crisis for tears, but her response need not have lacked sympathy. Carol's mother might have said to herself, "Carol is distressed. I can help her best by showing that I understand what pains her. How can I do that? *By reflecting her feelings to her.*" Thus she would have said one of the following:

"It will be lonely without Susie."

"You miss her already." ·

"It is hard to be apart when you are so used to being together."

"The house must seem kind of empty to you without Susie around."

Such responses create intimacy between parent and child. *When children feel understood, their loneliness and hurt diminish. When children are understood, their love for the parent is deepened. A parent's sympathy serves as emotional first aid for bruised feelings.*

When we genuinely *acknowledge a child's plight and voice her disappointment,* she often gathers the strength to face reality.

Seven-year-old Alice had made plans to spend the afternoon with her friend Lea. Suddenly, she remembered that her Brownie troop met that afternoon. She started to cry.

MOTHER: Oh, you're disappointed. You were looking forward to playing with Lea this afternoon.

ALICE: Yes. Why can't the Brownies meet another day?

The tears stopped. Alice called her friend Lea and made another appointment. She then proceeded to change her clothes and get ready for her Scout meeting.

Alice's mother's understanding and sympathizing with her daughter's disappointment helped Alice deal with life's inevitable conflicts and disappointments. She identified Alice's feelings and mirrored her wishes. She did not make light of the situation. She did not say: "Why do you make such a fuss! You'll play with Lea another day. What's the big deal?"

She deliberately avoided clichés: "Well, you can't be in two places at the same time." She neither accused nor blamed: "How come you made plans to play with a friend when you know that Wednesday is Brownie day?"

The following *brief* dialogue illustrates how this father reduced his son's anger by simply *acknowledging* his feelings and complaint.

When David's father, who has the night shift and takes care of the home while his wife works during the day, returned home from shopping, he found his eight-year-old in an angry mood.

FATHER: I see an angry boy. In fact, I see a very angry boy.

DAVID: I'm angry. In fact, I'm very angry.

FATHER: Oh?

DAVID: (*very quietly*) I missed you. You're never home when I come home from school.

FATHER: I'm glad you told me. Now I know. You want me to be home when you come home from school.

David hugged his father and went out to play. David's father knew how to change his son's mood. He did not become defensive by explaining why he wasn't home: "I had to go shopping. What would you eat if I did not buy food?" He did *not* ask: "Why are you so angry?" Instead, *he acknowledged his son's feelings and his complaint.*

Most parents are unaware that it is futile to try to convince children that their complaints are unjustified, their perceptions erroneous. It only leads to arguments and angry feelings.

One day, twelve-year-old Helen came home from school very upset.

HELEN: I know you'll be disappointed. I only got a B on my test. I know how important it is for you that I get an A.

MOTHER: But I really don't care. How can you even say such a thing? I'm not at all disappointed in your grade. I think a B is fine.

HELEN: Then why do you always yell at me when I don't get an A?

MOTHER: When did I yell at you? You're disappointed, so you're blaming me.

Helen started to cry and ran from the room. Even though Helen's mother understood that her daughter blamed her instead of acknowledging her own disappointment, pointing this out to her and arguing with her did not make her feel any better. Helen's mother would have been more helpful had she *acknowledged* her daughter's perception by saying: "You wish your grades were not that important to me. You want to be the one who decides what is a good grade for you. I see."

Not only children but even strangers appreciate our sympathetic understanding of their difficulties. Mrs. Grafton related that she dislikes going to her bank. "It's usually crowded and the manager looks and acts as if he's doing me a favor just being there. Whenever I have to approach him I become tense." One Friday she had to get his signature on a check. She was getting upset and impatient as she listened to his manner with others. But then she decided to try to put herself in his place and express her understanding *by reflecting and acknowledging his feelings.* "Another difficult Friday! Everyone's demanding your attention. It isn't even noon. I don't know how you manage to get through the day." The man's face lit up. For the first time she saw him smile. "Oh, yes, it's always busy here. Everyone wants to be taken care of first. And what can I do for you?" He not only signed the check, but walked with her to the teller to process it more quickly.

Fruitless Dialogues: Preaching and Criticizing Create Distance and Resentment

Parents are frustrated by dialogues with children because they lead nowhere, as illustrated by the famous conversation "Where did you go?" "Out." "What did you do?" "Nothing." Parents who try to be reasonable soon discover how exhausting this can be. As one mother said, "I try to reason with my child until I am blue in the face, but he doesn't listen to me. He only hears me when I scream."

Children often resist dialogues with parents. They resent being preached to, talked at, and criticized. They feel that parents talk too much. Says eight-year-old David to his mother, "When I ask you a small question, why do you give me such a long answer?" To his friends he confides, "I don't tell my mother anything. If I start in with her, I have no time left to play."

An interested observer who overhears a conversation between a parent and a child will note with surprise how little each listens to the other. The conversation sounds like two monologues, one consisting of criticism and instructions, the other of denials and pleading. The tragedy of such *communication* lies not in the lack of love, but in the lack of respect; not in the lack of intelligence, but in the lack of skill.

Our everyday language is not adequate for communicating meaningfully with children. To reach children and to reduce parental frustration, we need to learn a caring way of conversing with them.

Communication for Connection: Respond to Children's Feelings, Not Their Behavior

Communication with children should be based on respect and on skill; it requires (a) that messages preserve the child's as well as the parent's self-respect; and (b) that statements of understanding precede statements of advice or instruction.

Eric, age nine, came home full of anger. His class was scheduled to go for a picnic, but it was raining. His father decided to use a new approach. He refrained from clichés that in the past had only made things worse: "There is no use crying over bad weather. There will be other days for fun. I didn't make it rain, you know, so why are you angry at me?"

Instead Eric's father said to himself, My son has strong feelings about missing the picnic. He is disappointed. He is sharing his disappointment with me by showing me his anger. He is entitled to his emotions. I can best help him by showing *understanding and respect for his feelings.* To Eric he said, "You seem very disappointed."

ERIC: Yes.

FATHER: You wanted very much to go to this picnic.

ERIC: I sure did.

FATHER: You had everything ready and then the darn rain came.

ERIC: Yes, that's exactly right.

There was a moment of silence and then Eric said, "Oh, well, there will be other days." His anger seemed to have vanished and he was quite cooperative the rest of the afternoon. Usually when Eric came home angry, the whole household would be upset. Sooner or later he provoked every member of the family. Peace would not return until he was finally asleep late in the evening. What is so special about this approach, and what are its helpful components?

When children are in the midst of strong emotions, they cannot listen to anyone. They cannot accept advice or consolation or constructive criticism. *They want us to understand what is going on inside them, what they are feeling at that particular moment.* Furthermore, they want to be understood without having to disclose fully what they are experiencing. It is a game in which they reveal only a little of what they feel. We have to guess the rest.

When a child tells us, "The teacher yelled at me," we do not have to ask her for more details. Nor do we need to say, "What did you do to deserve it? If your teacher yelled at you, you must have done something. What did you do?" We don't even have to say, "Oh, I am so sorry." We need to show her that we understand her pain, her embarrassment, and her angry feelings.

Anita, age eight, came home for lunch one day, furious: "I'm not going back to school."

MOTHER: You seem quite upset. Would you like to tell me about it?

ANITA: The teacher ripped up my paper. I worked so hard on it and she just looked at it and ripped it up.

MOTHER: Without your permission? No wonder you're so angry!

Anita's mother refrained from any other comment or questions. She knew that her daughter needed her to talk to her with understanding and empathy if she was going to help diminish her daughter's rage.

Another example: Jeffrey, age nine, came home from school looking very unhappy, complaining: "The teacher made our day so hard."

MOTHER: You look tired out.

JEFFREY: Two kids were making noise in the library and she didn't know who they were, so she punished all of us by making us stay in the hall almost all day.

MOTHER: A whole class standing quietly in the hall all day instead of learning! No wonder you look tired.

JEFFREY: But I spoke to her. I said, "Ms. Jones, I have faith in your ability to find out who made the noise so you won't have to punish all of us."

MOTHER: My goodness, a nine-year-old young man helping his teacher to realize that it's not fair to punish a whole class for the misbehavior of a few!

JEFFREY: It didn't help. But at least she smiled for the first time that day.

MOTHER: Well, you didn't change her mind, but you sure changed her mood.

By *listening, respecting her son's feelings, acknowledging his perception*, and responding with appreciation to his attempt to be solution oriented, Jeffrey's mother helped him change his mood and diminish his anger.

How do we know what our children feel? We look at them and listen to them. We also draw on our own emotional experiences. We know what children *must* feel when they are shamed in public in the presence of peers. We phrase our words so that they know we understand what they have gone through. Any of the following statements would serve well:

> *"It must have been terribly embarrassing."*
> *"It must have made you furious."*
> *"You must have hated the teacher at that moment."*
> *"It must have hurt your feelings terribly."*
> *"It was a bad day for you."*

Unfortunately, when parents are confronted with children's misbehavior, they are unaware that usually disturbing feelings fuel that behavior. *Feelings must be dealt with before behavior can be improved.*

As twelve-year-old Ben's mother related, "I came home from work yesterday and before I had a chance to take off my coat, my son, Ben, rushed out of his bedroom and started to complain about his teacher: 'She gives so much homework, I couldn't get it done in a year. How am I going to write this poem by tomorrow morning? And I still owe a short story from last week. And today she screamed at me. She must really hate me!'

"I lost my cool and screamed at him, 'I have a boss that's just as mean as your teacher but you don't hear me complain. No wonder your teacher yells at you. You never get your homework done. You're just plain lazy. Stop complaining and start working or you'll fail.'"

"What happened after you expressed your anger?" I inquired.

"Well, my son stormed up to his room, locked the door, and wouldn't come down for supper."

"How did that make you feel?" I asked.

"Terrible. The whole evening was spoiled. Everyone was upset. The mood was depressing. I felt guilty but I didn't know what to do."

"How do you think your son felt?" I asked.

"Probably angry at me, frightened of his teacher, frustrated, hopeless, and too upset to concentrate. I was not much help to him. But I can't stand it when he complains and doesn't take responsibility."

Had Ben been able *to express his feelings, rather than complain*, this whole incident would have been avoided. Had he been able to say, "Mom, I'm scared to go to school tomorrow, I have to write a poem and a short story and I'm too upset to concentrate," his mother would then have been able to sympathize with her son by acknowledging his predicament: Starting with an emotional grunt, she could have paraphrased, "Hm, you're afraid you won't be able to write a poem and a short story before tomorrow morning. No wonder you feel overwhelmed."

Unfortunately, *neither we nor our children have been brought up to share our feelings. Often, we don't even know what or how we feel.*

Usually, when children find it difficult to cope, they become angry and blame others for their predicament, which usually enrages their parents, who then blame their children and say things they later regret, without solving the problem.

Since children find it difficult to share their feelings, it would be helpful if parents could learn to *hear the feelings of fear, despair, and helplessness that the angry outbursts hide.* Instead of *reacting* to the behavior, parents would *respond* to their children's upset feelings and help them cope. Only when children *feel right can they think clearly, and act right*—in this case concentrate, pay attention, and be able to listen.

Children's strong feelings do not disappear when they are told, "It is not nice to feel that way," or when parents try to convince them that they "have no reason to feel that way." *Strong feelings do not vanish by being banished;* but they do diminish in intensity and lose their sharp edges when the listener accepts them with sympathy and understanding.

This statement holds true not only for children but also for adults, as illustrated by the following excerpt from a parents' discussion group:

LEADER: Suppose it is one of those mornings when everything seems to go wrong. The telephone rings, the baby cries, and before you know it, the toast is burnt. Your spouse looks over the toaster and says: "My God! When will you learn to make toast?!" What is your reaction?

A: I would throw the toast in his face!

B: I would say, "Fix your own damn toast!"

C: I would be so hurt I could only cry.

LEADER: What would your spouse's words make you feel toward him or her?

PARENTS: Anger, hate, resentment.

LEADER: Would it be easy for you to fix another batch of toast?

A: Only if I could put some poison in it!

LEADER: And how would you feel about your day?

A: The whole day would be ruined!

LEADER: Suppose that the situation is the same: The toast is burnt. But your spouse, looking over the situation, says, "Gee, honey, it's a rough morning for you—the baby, the phone, and now the toast."

B: I would feel wonderful!

C: I would feel so good I would hug him and kiss him.

LEADER: Why? That baby is still crying and the toast is still burnt?

PARENTS: That wouldn't matter.

LEADER: What would make the difference?

A: You would feel grateful that you were not criticized.

LEADER: And what kind of day would you have?

C: A cheerful and happy one.

LEADER: Let me now give you a third scenario. Your spouse looks over the burnt toast and says to you calmly, "Let me show you, honey, how to make toast."

B: Oh, no. That's even worse than the first one. Now I'd feel stupid.

LEADER: Let's see how these three different approaches to the toast incident apply to our handling of children.

A: I see what you're driving at. I always say to my child, "You are old enough to know this, you are old enough to know that." It must make my child furious. It usually does.

B: I always say to my daughter, "Let me show you how to do this or that."

C: I'm so used to being criticized that it comes naturally to me. I use exactly the same words my mother used against me when I was a child. And I hated her for it. I never did anything right, and she always made me do things over.

LEADER: And you now find yourself using the same words with your daughter?

C: Yes. I don't like it at all. I don't like myself when I do.

LEADER: Let's see what we can learn from the burnt-toast story. What is it that helped change the mean feelings to loving ones?

B: The fact that somebody understood you.

C: Without blaming you.

A: And without telling you how to improve.

This vignette (adapted from Ginott, *Group Psychotherapy with Children* [McGraw-Hill, 1961]) illustrates the power of words to engender hostility or happiness. The moral of the story is that *our responses (words and feelings) can make a decided difference in the atmosphere of our homes.*

Principles of Conversation: Understanding and Empathy

When a child tells of, or asks about, an *event*, it is frequently best to respond not to the event, but to the *relationship* implied.

Flora, age six, complained that "lately" she had been receiving fewer presents than her brother. Her mother did not deny the complaint. Neither did she explain to Flora that her brother was older and so deserved more. Nor did she promise to right the wrong. She knew that children are more concerned about the depth of their relationships with parents than about the size and number of gifts. Her mother said, "You wonder if I love you as much as him?" Without adding another sentence, she embraced her Flora, who responded with a smile of surprise and pleasure. This was the end of a conversation that could have become an endless argument.

Behind many childhood questions is the desire for reassurance. The best answer for such questions is the assurance of our abiding relationship.

When a child tells of an *event,* it is sometimes helpful to respond not to the event itself, but to the *feelings* around it. Gloria, age seven, came home upset. She told her father how her girlfriend Dori was pushed off the sidewalk into a rain-filled gutter. Instead of asking for more details of the event or threatening to punish Dori's offenders, her father responded to his daughter's *feelings.* He said, "That must have upset you. You were angry at the boys who did it. You are still mad at them."

To all these statements, Gloria responded with an emphatic "Yes!" When her father said, "You're afraid that they may do it to you, too?" Gloria answered with determination: "Let them try, I'll drag them with me. That would make a splash!" Then she started to laugh at the picture in her mind. This was the happy ending of a conversation that could have become a sermon of useless advice on methods of self-defense.

When a child comes home with a host of complaints about a friend or a teacher or about his life, it is best to respond to the feeling tone, instead of trying to ascertain facts or to verify incidents.

Ten-year-old Harold came home cranky and complaining.

HAROLD: What a miserable life! The teacher called me a liar, just because I told her that I forgot the homework. And she yelled at me, did she yell! She said she'll write you a note.

MOTHER: You had a very rough day.

HAROLD: You can say that again.

MOTHER: It must have been terribly embarrassing to be called a liar in front of the whole class.

HAROLD: It sure was.

MOTHER: I bet inside yourself you wished her a few things!

HAROLD: Oh, yes! But how did you know?

MOTHER: That's what we usually do when someone hurts us.

HAROLD: That's a relief.

It is a deep comfort to children to discover that their feelings are a normal part of the human experience. There is no better way to convey that than to understand them.

When a child makes a statement about herself, it is often desirable to respond not with agreement or disagreement, but with specific details that convey to the child an understanding beyond expectation.

When a child says, "I am not good in arithmetic," it is of little help to tell her, "Yes, you are pretty lousy with figures." Nor is it helpful to dispute her opinion or to offer her cheap advice: "If you studied more, you would be better." Such hasty help only hurts her self-respect and the instant lesson only decreases her confidence.

Her statement "I am not good in arithmetic" can be met with earnestness and understanding. Any of the following would do:

"Arithmetic is not an easy subject."

"Some of the problems are very hard to figure out."

"The teacher does not make it easier with his criticism."

"Arithmetic makes you feel stupid."

"I bet you can't wait for the hour to pass."

"When it is over, you feel safer."

"Exam time must be extra tough."

"You must be worrying a lot about failing."

"You must be worrying about what we will think."

"You must be afraid we'll be disappointed in you."

"We know some subjects are not easy."

"We have faith that you'll do your best."

A twelve-year-old girl related that she almost fainted when her father talked to her with such understanding after she brought home a failing report card. Her inner reaction was, I must live up to my father's faith in me.

Once in a blue moon, almost every parent hears a son or daughter declare, "I am stupid." Knowing that *his* child cannot be stupid, the parent sets out to convince him that he is bright, as this father did.

CHARLES: I am stupid.

FATHER: You are not stupid.

CHARLES: Yes, I am.

FATHER: You are not. Remember how smart you were at camp? The counselor thought you were one of the brightest.

CHARLES: How do you know what he thought?

FATHER: He told me so.

CHARLES: Yeah, well, how come he called me stupid all the time?

FATHER: He was just kidding.

CHARLES: I am stupid, and I know it. Look at my grades in school.

FATHER: You just have to work harder.

CHARLES: I already work harder and it doesn't help. I have no brains.

FATHER: You are smart, I know.

CHARLES: I am stupid, I know.

FATHER (*loudly*): You are not stupid!

CHARLES: Yes I am!

FATHER: You are not stupid, Stupid!

When a child declares that he is stupid or ugly or bad, nothing that we can say or do will change his self-image immediately. A person's ingrained opinion of himself resists direct attempts at alteration. As one child said to his father, "I know you mean well, Dad, but I am not that stupid to take your word that I am bright."

When a child expresses a negative view of himself, our denials and protests are of little help to him. They bring forth only a stronger declaration of his convictions. *The best help we can offer is to show that we understand not only how this must make him feel, but its specific implications.* For example:

IVAN: I am stupid.

FATHER (*seriously*): You really feel that way, don't you? You don't think of yourself as smart?

IVAN: No.

FATHER: Then you suffer inside quite a lot?

IVAN: Yeah.

FATHER: In school, you must be afraid a great deal of the time, afraid you'll fail, afraid you'll get low marks. When the teacher calls on you, you get confused. Even when you know the answer, it doesn't come out right. You are afraid that your words will sound ridiculous . . . and that the teacher will criticize you . . . and that the children will laugh at you. So, many times you prefer to say nothing. I guess you can remember times when you said something and they laughed at you. It made you feel stupid in your own eyes. Hurt and angry, too. (*At this point the child may tell you of some of his experience.*)

FATHER: Look, Son! In my eyes you are a fine person. But you have a different opinion of yourself.

This conversation may not change the child's image of himself right then and there, but it may plant in him a seed of doubt about his inadequacy. He may think to himself, If my father understands me and considers me a fine person, perhaps I am not that worthless. The intimacy that such a conversation creates may lead the son to try to live up to his father's faith in him. Ultimately he will find more hopeful answers in himself.

When a child says, "I never have good luck," no argument or explanation will change her belief. For every instance of good fortune that we mention, she will respond with two tales of misfortune. All we can do is show her how intimately we understand the feelings that lead her to her belief:

ANNABELLE: I never have good luck.

MOTHER: You really feel that way?

ANNABELLE: Yes.

MOTHER: So when you play a game you think inside your-self, I'm not going to win. I don't have luck.

ANNABELLE: Yes, that's exactly what I think.

MOTHER: In school, if you know the answer you think, Today the teacher is not going to call on me.

DAUGHTER: Yes.

MOTHER: But if you didn't do the homework, you think, Today she is going to call on me.

ANNABELLE: Yes.

MOTHER: I guess you can give me many more examples.

ANNABELLE: Sure . . . like for instance (*child gives examples*).

MOTHER: I am interested in what you think about luck. If something happens that you think is bad luck, or even good luck, come and tell me and we'll talk about it.

This conversation may not change the child's belief in her bad luck. It may, however, convey to her how lucky she is to have such an understanding mother.

Fish Swim, Birds Fly, and People Feel: Mixed Feelings and Mixed Messages

Children love and resent us at the same time. They feel two ways about parents, teachers, and all persons who have authority over them. Parents find it difficult to accept ambivalence as a fact of life. They do not like it in them-selves and cannot tolerate it in their children. They think that there is something inherently wrong in feeling two ways about people, especially about members of the family.

We can learn to accept the existence of ambivalent feelings in ourselves and in our children. To avoid unnecessary conflicts, children need to know that such feelings are normal and natural. We can spare a child much guilt and anxiety by acknowledging and voicing those ambivalent feelings:

> *"You seem to feel two ways about your teacher: You like her and dislike her."*
>
> *"You seem to have two feelings about your older brother: You admire him, but you also resent him."*
>
> *"You have two thoughts on the subject: You would like to go to camp, but you also want to stay home."*

A calm, noncritical statement of their ambivalence is helpful to children because it conveys to them that even their "mixed-up" feelings are not beyond comprehension. As one child said, "If my mixed-up feelings can be understood, they are not so mixed up." On the other hand, statements such as the following are definitely not helpful: "Boy, are you mixed up! One minute you like your friend, and then you resent him. Make up your mind, if you have one."

A sophisticated view of human reality takes account of the possibility that where there is love, there is also some hate; where there is admiration, there is also some envy; where there is devotion, there is also some hostility; where there is success, there is also apprehension. It takes great wisdom to realize that *all feelings are legitimate: the positive, the negative, and the ambivalent.*

It is not easy to accept such concepts inwardly. Our childhood training and adult education predispose us to the opposite view. We have been taught that negative feelings are "bad" and should not be felt or that we should be ashamed of them. The new approach states that only real acts can be judged, while "bad" or "good" imaginary acts cannot be. Only *conduct* can be condemned or commended: *feelings* cannot and should not be. Judgment of feelings and censure of fantasy would do violence both to personal freedom and to mental health.

Emotions are part of our genetic heritage. *Fish swim, birds fly, and people feel.* Sometimes we are happy, sometimes we are not; but sometimes in our lives we are sure to *feel anger and fear, sadness and joy, greed and guilt, lust and scorn, delight and disgust.* While we are not free to choose the emotions that arise in us, we are free to choose how and when to express them, provided we know what they are. That is the crux of the problem. Many people have been educated out of knowing what their feelings are. When they felt hate, they were told it was only dislike. When they were afraid, they were told there was nothing to be afraid of. When they felt pain, they were advised to be brave and smile. Many of us have been taught to pretend to be happy when we're not.

What is suggested in the place of this pretense? *Truth.* Emotional education can help children to know what they feel. It is more important for a child to *know what she feels than why she feels it.* When she knows clearly what her feelings are, she is less likely to feel "all mixed-up" inside.

Mirroring Emotions: Reflecting Children's Feelings Helps Them to Understand How They Feel

Children learn about their physical likeness by seeing their image in a mirror. They learn about their emotional likeness by hearing their feelings reflected to them. The function of a mirror is to reflect an image as it is, without adding flattery or faults. We do not want a mirror to tell us, "You look terrible. Your eyes are bloodshot and your face is puffy. Altogether you are a mess. You'd better do something about yourself." After a few exposures to such a magic mirror, we would avoid it like the plague. *From a mirror we want an image, not a sermon.* We may not like the image we see; still, we would rather decide for ourselves our next cosmetic move.

Similarly, the function of an emotional mirror is to reflect feelings as they are, without distortion:

> *"It looks like you are very angry."*
> *"It sounds as if you hate him very much."*
> *"It seems as if you are disgusted with the whole situation."*

To a child who has such feelings, these statements are most helpful. They show clearly what his or her feelings are. Clarity of image, whether in a looking glass or in an emotional mirror, provides opportunity for self-initiated grooming and change.

As adults we have all felt hurt, angry, afraid, confused, or sad. *At times of strong emotion there is nothing as comforting and helpful as a person who listens and understands.*

What is true for adults is also true for children. Caring communication replaces criticism, lecturing, and advice with the healing balm of human understanding.

When one of our children is distressed, afraid, confused, or sad, we naturally rush in with judgment and advice. The clear, if unintended, message is: "You are too dull to know what to do." On top of the original pain we add the new insult.

There is a better way. When we offer the time and compassion to understand the child, we send a very different message: "You are important to me. I want to understand your feelings." Behind that vital message is the reassurance: "As you feel peaceful, you'll find the best solutions."

CHAPTER 2

The Power of Words:

Better Ways to Encourage and Guide

In psychotherapy, a child is never told, "You are a good little boy." "You are great." Judgmental and evaluative praise is avoided. Why? Because it is not helpful. It creates anxiety, invites dependency, and evokes defensiveness. It is not conducive to self-reliance, self-direction, and self-control, qualities that demand freedom from outside judgment. They require reliance on inner motivation and evaluation. *Children need to be free from the pressure of evaluative praise so that others do not become their source of approval.*

Isn't Praise Good for Children Anymore?

Sometimes misbehavior comes at the most unexpected times.

It was Monday morning after the Thanksgiving weekend. The family was in the car driving home from

Pittsburgh to New York. In the back of the car, Ivan, age six, behaved like an angel, quiet and deep in thought. His mother said to herself, He deserves some praise. They were just entering the Lincoln Tunnel when she turned to him and said, "You are such a good boy, Ivan. You behaved so well. I am proud of you."

A minute later Ivan pulled out an ashtray and spilled its contents all over his parents. The ashes and cigarette butts kept coming, like an atomic fallout. The family was in the tunnel, in heavy traffic, and were choking. Ivan's mother could have killed him. What upset her most was that she had just praised him. *Isn't praise good for children anymore?*, she asked herself.

Weeks later Ivan himself revealed the cause of the explosion. All the way home he had been wondering how he could get rid of his younger brother, who was snuggled up between his mother and father in the front of the car. Finally the idea occurred to him that if their car were jackknifed in the middle, he and his parents would be safe, but the baby would be cut in two. Just then his mother had congratulated him on his goodness. The praise made him feel guilty, and he wanted desperately to show that he did not deserve it. He looked around, saw the ashtray, and the rest had followed instantly.

Doing Something Well Does Not Turn You Into a Good Person

Most people believe that praise builds up children's confidence and makes them feel secure. In actuality, praise may result in tension and misbehavior. Why? Many children have, from time to time, destructive wishes about members of their family. When parents tell a child, "You are such a good boy," he may not be able to accept it because his own picture of himself is quite different. In his own eyes, he cannot be "good" when only recently he wished that his mother would disappear or that his brother would spend next weekend in the hospital. In fact, the more he is praised, the more he misbehaves in order to show his "true self." Parents frequently report that just after praising children for good behavior, they start to act wild, as though to disprove their compliment. It is possible that misbehaving is the child's way of communicating private reservations about a public image.

It is not unusual for children who are praised for being smart, to become *less* likely to take on challenging learning tasks since they do not want to risk their high standing. In contrast, *when children are praised for their efforts, they become more persistent in difficult tasks.*

Desirable and Undesirable Praise

Praise, like penicillin, must not be administered haphazardly. There are rules and cautions that govern the handling of potent medicines—rules about timing and dosage, cautions about possible allergic reactions. There are similar regulations about the administration of emotional medicine as well. The single most important rule is that *praise deal only with children's efforts and accomplishments, not with their character and personality.*

When a child cleans up the yard, it is only natural to comment on how hard she has worked, and on how good the yard looks. It is highly unrelated, and inappropriate, to tell her what a good person she is. *Words of praise should mirror for the child a realistic picture of her accomplishments, not a distorted image of her personality.*

The following example illustrates desirable praise: Julie, age eight, worked hard to clean up the yard. She raked the leaves, removed the garbage, and rearranged the tools. Mother was impressed and expressed her appreciation of her efforts and achievements:

MOTHER: The yard was so dirty. I didn't believe it could be cleaned up in one day.

JULIE: I did it!

MOTHER: It was full of leaves and garbage and things.

JULIE: I cleaned it all up.

MOTHER: You put in a lot of effort!

JULIE: Yeah, I sure did.

MOTHER: The yard is so clean now; it is a pleasure to look at it.

JULIE: It's nice.

MOTHER: Your beaming face tells me how proud you are. Thank you, dear.

JULIE (*with a mile-wide smile*): You're welcome.

Her mother's words made Julie feel glad of her efforts and proud of her accomplishments. That evening she could not wait for her father to come home in order to show him the cleaned-up yard and again to feel within herself the pride of a task well done.

In contrast, the following words of praise addressed to the child's personality are unhelpful:

"You are such a wonderful daughter."
"You are truly Mother's little helper."
"What would Mother do without you?"

Such comments may threaten a child and cause her anxiety. She may feel that she is far from being wonderful and that she is unable to live up to this label. So, instead of fearfully waiting to be exposed as a fraud, she may decide to lessen her burden immediately by a confession of misbehavior. Direct praise of personality, like direct sunlight, is uncomfortable and blinding. *It is embarrassing for a person to be told that she is wonderful, angelic, generous, and humble.* She feels called upon to deny at least part of the praise. Publicly, she cannot stand up and say, "Thank you, I accept your words that I am wonderful." Privately, too, she must reject such praise. She cannot honestly say to herself, I am wonderful. I am good and strong and generous and humble. She may not only reject the praise but may have some second thoughts about those who have praised her: If they find me so great, they cannot be so smart.

Learning the Process of Praise

Praise consists of two parts: what we say to children and what they in turn say to themselves.

Our words should state clearly what we like and appreciate about their effort, help, work, consideration, creation, or accomplishments. Our words should be framed so that a child will almost inevitably draw from them a realistic conclusion about his or her personality. Our words should be like a magic canvas upon which children cannot help but paint a positive picture of themselves.

Kenny, age eight, helped his father fix up the basement. In the process he had to move heavy furniture.

FATHER: The workbench is so heavy. It is hard to move.
KENNY (*with pride*): But I did it.
FATHER: It takes a lot of strength.
KENNY (*flexing his muscles*): I am strong.

In this example, Kenny's father commented on *the difficulty of the task*. It was Kenny himself who drew the inference about his personal power. Had his father said, "You are so strong, Son," Kenny might have replied, "No, I am not. There are stronger boys than I in my class." A fruitless, if not bitter, argument might have followed.

We usually praise our children when we want them to feel better about themselves. Why is it then that, when we say to our daughter, "You're beautiful!" she denies it. Why is it that, when we say to our son, "You're brilliant," he gets embarrassed and walks away? Is it that our children are so difficult to please that even praise does not help? Of course not. What is more likely is that our children, like most people, do not respond to words of praise that assess their personality or physical and mental attributes. Children do not like to be evaluated.

How would any of us feel if, at the end of each month, the person who claims to love us handed us an evaluation? "In kissing you get an A but in hugging you only get a B; in loving, on the other hand, you get an A+." We would be upset and feel degraded. We would not feel loved.

There is a better way: *description that details delight and admiration, words that convey recognition of effort, and statements that transmit respect and understanding.*

June, age thirteen, was alone in the house one evening when a burglar attempted to break in. She tried to call the neighbors, but no one answered. She then called the police.

When her parents returned home, they found a policeman taking testimony from June. Both Mother and Father were impressed with the mature manner that June handled the frightening incident.

But they did not praise her by telling her what a remarkable girl she was, nor how mature she was. Instead, they talked about the situation and described to her in detail and with great appreciation her effective behavior.

June's father said to her: "The way you acted fits Hemingway's definition of courage: 'Grace under pressure.' How impressive to see a thirteen-year-old keep her cool and in a hot situation, do what needs to be done to protect herself, call a neighbor, then call the police and give the necessary details. Your mom and I are filled with respect for you."

June listened as she started to relax. A big smile formed on her face and then she said: "I guess you can say that I'm learning to cope with life."

Because of her parents' response, June did not complain about being left alone. On the contrary, she came out of a frightening situation feeling more competent.

Here's another example: Lester's mother spent an afternoon watching her son play soccer. After the game, wanting to share with her son her appreciation of his skill and his accomplishment, she described in detail what impressed her: "It was such a pleasure to watch you play soccer this afternoon, especially the last ten seconds when you saw an opportunity to score. You ran all the way down to the other end of the field from your defensive position and set up the winning goal. You must be so proud!"

She added "*You* must be so proud" because she wanted him to develop an inner pride.

A father asked his six-year-old daughter, Jennifer, to help him pile the leaves after he had raked them. When they were finished, the father pointed to the piles and said, "One, two, three, four, five, six! Six piles in thirty minutes! How did you ever manage to work so fast?" That evening as Jennifer was saying good night to her father, she asked, "Daddy, can you tell me again about my piles?"

It takes effort to be specific and descriptive in our praise. Children benefit from the information and appreciation much more than when we evaluate their character.

George's mother left this note on her son's guitar: "Your playing gives me great pleasure." Her son was delighted. "Thanks for saying what a good player I am." He translated his mother's appreciation into a statement that sang his praise.

Praise can also be discouraging. It depends on what the child says to herself after she is praised.

When twelve-year-old Linda arrived at the third level of her videogame, her father exclaimed, "You're great! You have perfect coordination! You're an expert player." Linda lost interest and walked away. Her father's praise made it difficult for her to continue because she said to herself, "Dad thinks I'm a great player, but I'm no expert. I made the third level by luck. If I try again, I may not even make the second level. It is better to quit while I'm ahead." It would have been more helpful for her father to simply observe, "It must feel great to reach a new level."

The following examples further illustrate this point:

Helpful praise: Thank you for washing the car; it looks new again.

Possible inference: I did a good job. My work is appreciated.

(Unhelpful praise: You are an angel.)

Helpful praise: I liked your get-well card. It was so pretty and witty.

Possible inference: I have good taste. I can rely on my choices.

(Unhelpful praise: You are *always* so considerate.)

Helpful praise: Your poem spoke to my heart.

Possible inference: I am glad I can write poems.

(Unhelpful praise: You are a good poet for your age.)

Helpful praise: The bookcase that you built looks beautiful.

Possible inference: I am capable.

(Unhelpful praise: You are such a good carpenter.)

Helpful praise: Your letter brought me great joy.

Possible inference: I can bring happiness to others.

(Unhelpful praise: You are an excellent writer.)

Helpful praise: I appreciate greatly your washing the dishes today.

Possible inference: I am responsible.

(Unhelpful praise: You did a better job than anyone.)

Helpful praise: Thanks for telling me that I overpaid you. I appreciate it very much.

Possible inference: I'm glad I was honest.

(Unhelpful praise: You are such an honest child.)

Helpful praise: Your composition gave me several new ideas.

Possible inference: I can be original.

(Unhelpful praise: You write well for your grade. Of course, you still have a lot to learn.)

Such descriptive statements and children's positive conclusions are the building blocks of mental health. What they conclude about themselves in response to our words, children later restate silently to themselves. Realistic positive statements repeated inwardly by children determine to a large extent their good opinion of themselves and of the world around them.

Providing Your Child with Guidance Rather Than Criticism

Criticism and evaluative praise are two sides of the same coin. Both are judgmental. To avoid being judgmental, psychologists do not use criticism to influence children. *They use guidance.* In criticism parents attack children's personality attributes and their character. *In guidance we state the problem and a possible solution. We say nothing to the child about himself or herself.*

When eight-year-old Mary accidentally spilled her juice, her mother commented calmly, "I see the juice spilled. Let's get another glass of juice, and a sponge." She got up and handed the juice and the sponge to her daughter. Mary looked up at her in relief and disbelief. She muttered, "Gee, thanks, Mom." She cleaned up the table while her mother helped her. She did not add cutting comments or useless admonitions. Mary's mother related, "I was tempted to say, 'Next time be careful,' but when I saw how grateful she was for my benevolent silence, I said nothing."

When things go wrong is not the right time to teach an offender about his personality. When things go wrong, it is best to deal only with the *event*, not with the *person.*

Imagine that you are driving with your beloved and make a wrong turn. Would it be helpful for him or her to say, "Why did you take the wrong turn? Didn't you see the sign? There's a big sign back there. Anyone can see it." At that moment would you feel a great surge of love? Would you say to yourself, I'm going to improve my driving and reading because I want to please my beloved? Or would you be tempted to respond in kind? What would be helpful? A sympathetic emotional sigh: "Oh, honey, how frustrating!" Or maybe just simple information: "There's an exit eleven miles from here."

When Things Go Wrong, Respond Rather Than React

In many homes, storms between parents and children develop in a regular and predictable sequence. The child does or says something "wrong." The parent reacts with something insulting. The child replies with something worse. The parent retorts with high-pitched threats or with high-handed punishment. And the free-for-all is on.

During breakfast one morning Nathaniel, age seven, was playing with an empty cup while his father was reading the paper.

FATHER: You'll break it. You are always breaking things.
NATHANIEL: No, I won't.

Just then the cup fell on the floor and broke.

FATHER: For crying out loud, you are so stupid. You break everything in the house.
NATHANIEL: You're stupid, too. You broke Mom's best plate.
FATHER: You called your father stupid! You're rude!
NATHANIEL: You are rude. You called me stupid first.
FATHER: Not another word from you! Go up to your room immediately!
NATHANIEL: Go ahead, make me!

At this direct challenge to his authority, the father became enraged. He grabbed his son and started spanking him in fury. While attempting to escape, Nathaniel pushed his father into a glass door. The glass broke and cut his father's hand. The sight of blood threw Nathaniel into a panic. He ran out of the house and was not found until late in the evening. The whole household was upset and no one in the house slept well that night.

Whether or not Nathaniel learned to avoid empty cups was less important than the negative lesson that he learned about himself and his father. The question is, Was this battle necessary? Was the fighting inevitable? Or is it possible to handle such incidents more wisely?

Upon seeing his son playing with the cup, the father could have removed it and directed him to a more suitable substitute, such as a ball. Or when the cup broke, he could have helped his son dispose of the pieces, with comments such as "Cups can break so easily. Who would have thought that such a small cup could make such a big mess?"

The surprise of such a low-toned sentence might have sent Nathaniel into atonement and apology for the mishap. In the absence of screams and spankings, he may even have had the presence of mind to conclude for himself that cups are not for playing.

Minor mishaps and major values. From minor mishaps children can learn major lessons in values. Children need to learn from their parents to distinguish between events that are merely unpleasant and annoying and those that are tragic or catastrophic. Many parents react to a broken egg as to a broken leg, to a shattered window as to a shattered heart. Minor misfortunes should be pointed out as such to children: "So you lost your glove again. That is annoying. It's regrettable, but it is not a catastrophe. It's only a mishap."

A lost glove need not lead to a lost temper; a torn shirt need not serve as a prop for a do-it-yourself Greek tragedy.

On the contrary, a mishap can be a good time to teach values. When eight-year-old Diana lost the birthstone in her ring, she started to cry bitterly. Her father looked at her and said clearly and forcefully, "In our home stones are not that important. People are important. Feelings are important. Anyone can lose a stone, but stones can be replaced. It's your feelings that matter to me. You really like that ring. I hope you find the stone."

Parental criticism is unhelpful. It creates anger and resentment. Even worse, children who are regularly criticized learn to condemn themselves and others. They learn to doubt their own worth and to belittle the value of others. They learn to suspect people and to expect personal doom.

Eleven-year-old Justin promised to wash the family car. He forgot to do it. He made a last-minute attempt to do the job but didn't finish it.

FATHER: The car needs more work, Son, especially on the top and the left side. When can you do it?

JUSTIN: I can work on the car tonight, Dad.

FATHER: Thank you.

Instead of criticism, this father gave his son *information without derogation,* making it possible for the son to finish the job without getting angry with his father. Imagine how differently Justin would have reacted if his father had used criticism in an effort to educate his son:

FATHER: Did you wash the car?

JUSTIN: Yes, Dad.

FATHER: Are you sure?

JUSTIN: I'm sure.

FATHER: You call that washing? You played at it as you always do. Fun, that's all you want. You think you can get through life like that? With such sloppy work you won't last one day on a job. You're irresponsible, that's what you are!

Nine-year-old Barbara's mother did not know how to respond to her daughter, either, without criticizing.

When Barbara came home hysterical from school one day complaining, "Everything happened to me today; my books fell into a puddle; the boys kept picking on me; and somebody stole my sneakers," her mother, instead of sympathizing with her daughter, admonished and criticized her: "Why does everything happen to you? Why can't you be like other children? What's wrong with you?" Barbara started to cry. What would have helped Barbara feel better? A simple sympathetic acknowledgment of her difficult day: "Oh, honey, you sure had an unusually rough day!"

Abusive Adjectives Harm Our Children

Abusive adjectives, like poisonous arrows, are not to be used against children. When a person says, "This is an ugly chair," nothing happens to the chair. It is neither insulted nor embarrassed. It stays just as it is regardless of the adjective attached to it. However, when children are called ugly or stupid or clumsy, something does happen to them. There are reactions in their bodies and in their souls. Resentment, anger, and hate develop. Fantasies of revenge emerge. Undesirable behavior and troublesome symptoms may surface. Verbal attacks generate a chain of reactions that makes children and their parents miserable.

When a child is called clumsy, he may at first retort with "No, I am not clumsy." But, more often than not, he believes his parents, and he comes to think of himself as a clumsy person. When he happens to stumble or to fall, he may say aloud to himself, "You are so clumsy!" From then on, he may avoid situations in which agility is required because he is convinced that he is too clumsy to succeed.

When a child is repeatedly told by her parents or teachers that she is stupid, she comes to believe it. She starts thinking of herself as such. She then gives up intellectual efforts, feeling that her escape from ridicule lies in avoiding contest and competition. Her safety hinges on not trying. Her motto in life becomes: "If I don't try, I can't fail."

Isn't it amazing how many negative and demeaning comments parents make in the presence of their children without realizing their hurtful and destructive consequences? For example:

> "From the moment he was born he was nothing but trouble and he's been nothing but trouble ever since."
>
> "She's just like her mother. Stubborn. She does what she wants. We have no control over her."
>
> "All she know is gimme, gimme. But she's never satisfied, no matter how much you give her."
>
> "That sweet little boy takes every moment of my day. He's so irresponsible. I have to watch him like a hawk."

Unfortunately, children take these remarks seriously. Little children especially depend on their parents to tell them who they are and what they are capable of becoming. For children to develop a worthwhile sense of themselves, they need to hear and overhear mostly positive remarks about themselves.

It's ironic that many parents find it easier to point out what's wrong with their children than what's right with them. *Yet, if we want our children to grow up feeling confident and self-assured, we need to take every opportunity to emphasize the positive and avoid demeaning comments.*

Congruent Communication: Have the Words Fit the Feelings

Children can irritate and infuriate. Yet we try hard to be patient and understanding. Inevitably we run out of steam and explode, perhaps about a child's room: "You're not even fit to live in a pigsty!" Then full of remorse we try to apologize: "I didn't mean it. You are fit to live in a pigsty."

We would like to believe that patience is a virtue. But is it? Not if it demands that we pretend to be calm when we feel agitated, that we not act the way we feel, that our behavior, instead of reflecting, hides our true feelings.

Having been brought up not to show our true emotions, we are proudest when, in the midst of the greatest turmoil, we show the least reaction. Some call it patience.

But what children need from their parents and appreciate is a *congruent response*. They want to hear *words that reflect parents' true feelings.*

It's not unusual even for a small child to protect himself or herself from parental anger by hurling the most potent of all accusations: "You don't love me." "But of course I love you!" yells the parent in a tone so angry that it belies the words without reassuring the child. Parents don't feel loving when angry. By invoking love the child has put the parent on the defensive, cleverly shifting the focus from herself to the parent.

Only parents who give themselves permission not to feel loving when angry can answer a child's accusation without becoming defensive: "This is not a good time to talk about love, but it is a good time to talk about what made me angry."

The angrier the parent, the greater the child's need to be reassured. But expressing love in an angry tone is not comforting. It does not make a child feel loved. It only creates confusion because what a child hears are not loving words, but the anger that the abrasive voice conveys. It's more helpful for children to learn that anger does not lead to abandonment. The loss of loving feelings is only temporary; they will reappear as soon as the anger disappears.

Handling Our Own Anger

In our own childhood, we were not taught how to deal with anger as a fact of life. We were made to feel guilty for experiencing anger and sinful for expressing it. We were led to believe that to be angry is to be bad. Anger was not merely a misdemeanor; it was a felony. With our own children, we try to be patient; in fact, so patient that sooner or later we must explode. We are afraid that our anger may be harmful to children, so we hold it in, as a skin diver holds his breath. In both instances, however, the capacity for holding in is rather limited.

Anger, like the common cold, is a recurrent problem. We may not like it, but we cannot ignore it. We may know it intimately, but we cannot prevent its appearance. Anger arises in predictable sequences and situations, yet it always seems sudden and unexpected. And, though it may not last long, anger seems eternal for the moment.

When we lose our temper, we act as though we have lost our sanity. We say and do things to our children that we would hesitate to inflict on an enemy. We yell, insult, and attack. When the fanfare is over, we feel guilty and we solemnly resolve never to render a repeat performance. But anger inevitably strikes again, undoing our good intentions. Once more we lash out at those to whose welfare we have dedicated our life and fortune.

Resolutions about not becoming angry are worse than futile. They only add fuel to fire. Anger, like a hurricane, is a fact of life to be acknowledged and prepared for. The peaceful home, like the hoped-for peaceful world, does not depend on a sudden benevolent change in human nature. It does depend on *deliberate procedures that methodically reduce tensions before they lead to explosions.*

Emotionally healthy parents are not saints. They're aware of their anger and respect it. They use their anger as a source of information, an indication of their caring. *Their words are congruent with their feelings.* They do not hide their feelings. The following episode illustrates how a mother encouraged cooperation by venting her anger without insulting or humiliating her daughter.

Jane, age eleven, came home screaming: "I can't play baseball. I don't have a shirt!" The mother could have given her daughter an acceptable solution: "Wear your blouse." Or, wanting to be helpful, she could have helped Jane look for the shirt. Instead, she decided to express her true feelings: "I'm angry, I'm mad. I've bought you six baseball shirts and they're either mislaid or lost. Your shirts belong in your dresser. Then, when you need them, you'll know where to find them."

Jane's mother expressed her anger without insulting her daughter, as she commented later: "Not once did I bring up past grievances or reopen old wounds. Nor did I call my daughter names. I did not tell her she's a scatterbrain and irresponsible. I *just described how I felt and what needed to be done in the future to avoid unpleasantness.*"

Her mother's words helped Jane herself come up with a solution. She hurried off to search for the mislaid shirts at her friend's house and in the locker room in the gym.

There is a place for parental anger in child education. In fact, failure to get angry at certain moments would only convey to the child indifference, not goodness. Those who care cannot altogether shun anger. This does not mean that children can withstand floods of fury and violence; it means only that they can stand and understand anger that says, "There are limits to my tolerance."

For parents, anger is a costly emotion: To be worth its price, it should not be employed without profit. Anger should not be used so that it increases with expression. The medication must not be worse than the disease. *Anger should be expressed in a way that brings some relief to the parent, some insight to the child, and no harmful side effects to either of them.* Thus we should not bawl out children in front of their friends; it only makes them act up more, which in turn makes us angrier. We are not interested in creating or perpetuating waves of anger, defiance, retaliation, and revenge. On the contrary, we want to get our point across and let the stormy clouds evaporate.

Three Steps to Survival

To prepare ourselves in times of peace to deal with times of stress, we should acknowledge the following truths:

1. We accept the fact that we will sometimes get angry in dealing with children.
2. We are entitled to our anger without guilt or shame.
3. Except for one safeguard, we are entitled to express what we feel. *We can express our angry feelings provided we do not attack the child's personality or character.*

These assumptions should be implemented in concrete procedures for dealing with anger. The first step in handling turbulent feelings is to identify them clearly by name. This gives a warning to whomever it may concern to make amends or to take precautions. We do this by starting with the pronoun *I*: "I feel annoyed." Or "I feel irritated."

If our short statements and long faces have not brought relief, we proceed to the second step. We express our anger with increasing intensity:

"I feel angry."
"I feel very angry."
"I feel very, very angry."
"I feel furious."

Sometimes the mere statement of our feelings (without explanations) stops the child from misbehaving. At other times it may be necessary to proceed to the third step, which is to give the reason for our anger, to state our inner reactions and our *wishful* actions:

*"When I see the shoes and the socks and the shirts and
the sweaters spread all over the floor, I get angry, I
get furious. I feel like opening the window and
throwing the whole mess into the middle of the
street."*

*"It makes me angry to see you hit your brother. I get so
mad inside myself that I see red. I start boiling. I
can never allow you to hurt him."*

*"When I see all of you rush away from dinner to watch
TV, and leave me with the dirty dishes and greasy
pans, I feel indignant! I get so mad, I fume inside! I
feel like taking all the dishes and breaking them on
the TV set!"*

*"When I call you for dinner and you don't come, I
get angry. I get very angry. I say to myself, 'I cooked
a good meal and I want some appreciation, not
frustration!'"*

This approach allows parents to vent their anger without causing damage. On the contrary, it may even illustrate an important lesson in how to express anger safely.
The child may learn that his or her own anger is not catastrophic, that it can be discharged without destroying anyone. This lesson will require more than just expression of
anger by parents. It will require that parents point out to
their children acceptable channels of emotional expression and demonstrate to them safe and respectable ways
of expressing anger.

Spouses also appreciate anger without insult. A father
related the following: "As I was leaving for work one
morning, my wife informed me that our nine-year-old son,
Harold, while playing ball in the living room, had broken

the glass of the antique wall clock for the second time. I became angry, forgot all I had learned, and lashed out, 'Obviously, you have no regard for our things! Wait until I get home this evening. I will punish you so hard that you will never dare to play ball in the living room!' My wife walked me to the door and, not realizing that labeling is just as disabling and enraging for husbands as it is for children, she said to me: 'Boy, what a stupid thing to say to Harold!' Since I love my wife, I suppressed my anger and answered, 'I guess you're right.' At first I was angry only at my son. After my wife called me stupid, I also became enraged at her. I already felt guilty for reverting to my old way of talking. I did not need her to rub it in. How much more helpful it would have been had she said to me, 'It's infuriating to have the glass broken twice. I wonder how we can help Harold avoid this incident in the future.'"

Melissa's father was more fortunate. His wife knew how to influence him without enraging. Seven-year-old Melissa and her parents were riding in a car one evening when the following conversation took place:

MELISSA: What does pizza mean?

FATHER: Pizza? It's an Italian word for pie.

MELISSA: What does pharmacy mean?

FATHER: It's another word for drugstore.

MELISSA: What does bank mean?

FATHER (*getting angry*): You know that one. It's a place where people keep their money.

MELISSA: How does day turn into night?

FATHER (*very angry*): Boy, you sure ask a lot of questions. When the sun goes down there is no more light.

MELISSA: Why is the moon moving with the car?

MOTHER: What an interesting question! Do you know that this question has puzzled scientists for hundreds of years and so they decided to study the movement of the moon?

MELISSA (*excited*): Boy, then I'm going to be a scientist. I'm going to the library and find a book that tells me all about the moon.

The questions stopped. This mother understood that to keep answering children's questions only encourages them to ask more questions. But she resisted the temptation to point this out to her husband. Instead, she *demonstrated* that by not giving her daughter a direct answer, she helped her find her own way of satisfying her curiosity.

Chris' mother, who had been trying to discourage her husband from ordering his children around, shared the following incident: One evening while she and her husband were enjoying a glass of wine in the kitchen of their beach house, her husband noticed a beach bag, a wet bathing suit, and a beach ball on the table. His usual response was to get angry and bark at the children like a drill sergeant in the army: "How many times do I have to tell you to put your things away! You're so inconsiderate! What do you think we are, slaves to pick up after you?"

But this time he calmly described what he saw: "I see a beach bag, a wet bathing suit, and a beach ball on the kitchen table." Eight-year-old Chris jumped up from his seat in the living room and exclaimed: "Oh, that must be mine," as he went into the kitchen to pick up his things.

After Chris left, his father said to his mother gleefully, "I remembered and it works!"

"Instead of saying, 'I told you so,' I lifted my glass in a toast to words that invite children's cooperation."

Responding to an Angry Child: The Method Is the Message

When children get upset, they cannot be reached by reasoning. When angry, they respond only to emotional balm.

Two young siblings were playing in the basement. Suddenly a noise of destruction, followed by shouting and accusations, was heard. Red with anger, Billy, age six, ran up the stairs and blurted out, "Betsy knocked over my fort." His mother sympathized: "Oh-h-h-h, that must have made you very angry." "It sure did." He turned around and went back to play.

This was the first time Billy's mother managed not to get involved in her children's daily scraps. By not asking the fatal question "Who started it?" she avoided her son's usual recital of grievances and requests for revenge. *By mirroring his inner mood,* she avoided the disagreeable role of becoming judge, prosecutor, and law enforcer to her children.

In the following episode, a mother's empathic comment made a difference between peace and war. Nine-year-old David did not want to go to the dentist. He was angry and irritating his older sister, Tina, who said to him, "Oh, David, grow up!" David became angrier and nastier.

Her mother turned to Tina and said, "David is upset today. He's worried about his visit to the dentist. Right now he needs all our consideration." As if by magic, David quieted down. He went to the dentist without further complaints. By *responding to David's upset feelings,* rather than to his irritating behavior, Mother made it possible for him to feel more relaxed and thus less obnoxious.

This vignette contrasts two ways of helping small children defuse their anger and tolerate frustration. One escalates the anger; the other diminishes it.

Tom and his friend Jim, both three-year-olds, were playing with toy xylophones. When Jim's hammer got stuck, he got angry and started to cry. His mother admonished him: "That's no reason to carry on. I won't fix it until you stop screaming." Jim continued to cry and his mother took away his toy. The resulting temper tantrum was a sight to behold.

In contrast, when Tom's hammer got stuck, and he started to cry, his mother said to him, "You're crying because the hammer is stuck. We need to fix it." The crying stopped. Now whenever the hammer gets stuck, Tom no longer cries, but brings it to his mother to fix.

Jim's mother scolded, threatened, blamed, and punished while Tom's mother *defined the problem and suggested a solution.*

Miriam, age twelve, returned from the theater disgruntled and angry:

MOTHER: You look unhappy.

MIRIAM: I'm furious! I had to sit so far back that I couldn't see anything of the play.

MOTHER: No wonder you're upset. It's no fun when you sit so far back.

MIRIAM: It sure wasn't. Besides, there was a tall guy sitting in front of me.

MOTHER: That's adding insult to injury. All the way back and behind a tall person! That's too much!

MIRIAM: It sure was.

The helpful ingredient in Miriam's mother's response was her acceptance of Miriam's mood without criticism or advice. She did not ask unhelpful questions, such as,

"Why didn't you go earlier to get a better seat?" or "Couldn't you ask the tall man to change seats with you?" She concentrated on helping her daughter diminish her anger.

An empathic response that mirrors to children their upset feelings and expresses the parents' sympathy and understanding is effective in changing children's angry moods.

The written word can be a powerful tool for restoring damaged feelings that result from angry outbursts. Both children and parents need to be encouraged to express their feelings in writing, be it an e-mail or a letter.

One evening, thirteen-year-old Trudy hurled insults at her mother, accusing her of going into her room, unlocking her desk, and reading her diary. When she realized that her suspicion was groundless, Trudy decided to apologize in writing:

Dear Mom, I have just committed the worst crime a moral person can commit. I made my mother unhappy and miserably upset with my accusation. I'm ashamed and humiliated. I used to feel good about myself but now I hate myself. I love you, Trudy

Trudy's mother was upset when the note made her realize that the incident shattered Trudy's positive self-image. She took time to compose a letter that would restore Trudy's loving self.

Dearest Trudy, Thank you for sharing your troubled and unhappy feelings with me. What happened the other evening was difficult for both of us, but not tragic. I want you to know that my feelings about you and for you have in no way changed. I see you as the same lovable person who at times can get very upset and angry. I hope you will find it in your heart to forgive yourself, to recapture the good feelings about yourself. Much love, Your Mom

The mother was helpful in reassuring her daughter that *getting angry need not alter one's loving feelings for oneself or others.*

Often after getting angry at their parents for not listening to their argument, children will present their case in writing.

A father related the following incident. In his home the children are given certificates that they may cash in for extra time at night before going to sleep. One evening, Peter, age ten, wanted to buy some time with a certificate, which he had lost. His father refused to honor a nonexistent certificate. Peter became frustrated and angry, screaming as he ran out of the room, "But you gave it to me!" When Peter's father went to his bedroom that evening he found the following letter:

Dear Dad, If you do not let me stay up, you are not being just because (1) we both know that you gave me the certificate, (2) you know what my desk is like and I lose things, (3) you know how much I was looking forward to using the certificate. I don't want to seem obnoxious for writing this. I'm only stating my own mind. XXX Peter

When the father read the note, he realized that Peter was showing him a way to repair the bad feelings between them. It also gave him an opportunity to try an important child-rearing principle. *Whenever possible enhance your child's self-worth.* He therefore penned the following note.

Dear Son, What clarity of thought! What persuasive arguments! As I was reading it, I had to remind myself that it was not written by a young man much older than ten. Enclosed please find the replaced certificate. Love, Dad

Summary

Words have the power to build and energize or to frighten and devastate. When we notice and appreciate children's efforts, we help them grow in hope and confidence. In contrast, when we evaluate the child, we activate anxiety and resistance. It may seem obvious that negative labels ("lazy," "stupid," "mean") are damaging to children; it comes as a surprise that even positive labeling ("good," "perfect," "best") can be disabling.

It is important that we be positive and encouraging with children. We acknowledge effort and express appreciation ("You worked very hard on that." "Thank you for your help."), but we do not label or evaluate the child.

When there are problems, we look for solutions rather than blame or criticize. Even the inevitable anger can be expressed without labeling or blaming. Behind all these skills of caring communication is a deep respect for children.

CHAPTER 3

Self-defeating Patterns:

There's No Right Way to Do a Wrong Thing

Certain patterns of relating to children are almost always self-defeating; not only do they fail to attain our long-term goals, but they often create havoc at home here and now. The self-defeating patterns include threats, bribes, promises, sarcasm, verbal overkill, sermons on lying and stealing, and rude teaching of politeness.

Threats: Invitations to Misbehavior

To children, threats are invitations to repeat a forbidden act. When a child is told, "If you do it once more," he does not hear the words "if you." He hears only "do it once more." Sometimes he interprets it as, Mom expects me to do it once more, or she'll be disappointed. Such warnings—fair as they may seem to adults—are worse than useless. They make sure that an obnoxious act will be repeated. *A warning serves as a challenge to the child's autonomy.* If he has any self-respect, he must transgress again, to show to himself and to others that he is not afraid to respond to a dare.

Oliver, age five, kept on throwing a ball at the living room window in spite of many warnings. Finally his father said, "If the ball hits the window once more, I'll beat the living daylights out of you. I promise." A minute later, the crash of breaking glass told Oliver's father that his warning had an effect: The ball had hit the glass for the last time. The scene that followed this sequence of threats, promises, and misbehavior can easily be imagined. In contrast, the following incident is an illustration of effective handling of misbehavior without resorting to threats.

Seven-year-old Peter shot the popgun at his baby brother. His mother said, "Not at the baby. Shoot at the target." Peter shot at the baby again. His mother took the gun away. To Peter she said, "People are not for shooting."

Peter's mother did what she felt had to be done to protect the baby and at the same time uphold her standards of acceptable behavior. Her son learned the consequences of his actions without any damage to his ego. The implied alternatives were obvious: to shoot at the target or to lose the privilege of having the gun. In this incident, his mother avoided the usual pitfalls. She did not embark on the predictable trail to failure: "Stop it, Peter! Don't you know better than to shoot at your brother? Don't you have a better target? If you do it once more, you hear, once more, you'll never see the gun again!" Unless the child is very meek, his response to such an admonition will be a repetition of the forbidden. The scene that would then follow need not be described—it can easily be reconstructed by every parent.

Bribes: Rethinking the "If-Then" Fallacy

Similarly self-defeating is the approach that explicitly tells a child that *if* he will (or will not) do something, *then* he will get a reward:

> "If *you are nice to your baby brother,* then *I'll take you to the movies."*
>
> "If *you stop wetting your bed,* then *I'll get you a bicycle for Christmas."*
>
> "If *you learn the poem,* then *I'll take you sailing."*

This "if-then" approach may occasionally spur the child toward an immediate goal. But it seldom, if ever, inspires her toward continual efforts. Our very words convey to her that we doubt her ability to change for the better. "If you learn the poem" means "We are not sure you can." "If you stop wetting" means "We think you can control yourself but you won't."

There are also some moral objections to rewards that are used to bribe. Some children purposely misbehave in order to get their parents to pay them to behave better. Such reasoning may soon lead to bargaining and blackmail, and to ever-increasing demands for prizes and fringe benefits in exchange for "good" behavior. Some parents have been so conditioned by their children that they do not dare come home from a shopping trip without a present. They are greeted by the children not with a "Hello," but with a "What-did-you-bring-me?"

Rewards are most helpful and more enjoyable when they are unannounced in advance, when they come as a surprise, when they represent recognition and appreciation.

Promises: Why Unrealistic Expectations Cause Grief for Everyone

Promises should neither be made to, nor demanded of, children. Why such a taboo on promises? Relations with our children should be built on trust. *When parents must make promises to emphasize that they mean what they say, then they are as much as admitting that their "unpromised" word is not trustworthy.* Promises build up unrealistic expectations in children. When a child is promised a visit to the zoo, she considers it a commitment that the day will not be rainy, that the car will be in the garage, and that she will not be sick. Since life is not without mishaps, however, children come to feel betrayed and convinced that parents cannot be trusted. The relentless complaint "But you promised!" is painfully familiar to parents who belatedly wish they had not.

Promises about future good behavior or the cessation of past misbehavior should not be requested or extracted from children. When a child makes a promise that is not her own, she draws a check on a bank in which she has no account. We should not encourage such fraudulent practices.

Sarcasm: A Sound Barrier to Learning

A serious mental health hazard is a parent with a gift for sarcasm. A wizard with words, that parent erects a sound barrier to effective communication:

"How many times must I repeat the same thing? Are you deaf? Then why don't you listen?"

"You are so rude. Were you brought up in a jungle? That's where you belong, you know."

"What's the matter with you, anyhow? Are you crazy or just stupid? I know where you'll end up!"

Such a parent may not even be aware that the remarks are attacks that invite counterattacks, that such comments block communication by stirring children to preoccupation with revenge fantasies. *Bitter sarcasm and cutting clichés have no place in child upbringing.* It is best to avoid statements such as "What makes you think you know all the answers? You don't even have the brains you were born with. You think you're so smart!" Wittingly or unwittingly, we should not deflate the child's status in his own eyes and in the eyes of his peers.

Authority Calls for Brevity: When Less Is More

To be told "You talk like a parent" is not a compliment, because parents have a reputation for repeating themselves and overstating the obvious. When they do, children stop listening with a silent cry: "Enough already!"

Every parent needs to learn *economical* methods of responding to children, so that minor mishaps do not turn into major catastrophes. The following episode illustrates the triumph of a brief comment over a long explanation.

As Al's mother was saying good-bye to visitors in the driveway, eight-year-old Al ran up with a long tearful complaint against his older brother: "Whenever I have a friend over, Ted finds an excuse to tease us. He never leaves us alone. You have to stop him."

In the past, Al's mother would have yelled at Ted: "How many times do I have to tell you to leave your brother alone? So help me, if you don't, I'm going to ground you for a month."

This time she looked at Ted and said, "Ted, you choose. You can get the usual lecture or take care of the complaint yourself." Ted laughed and answered, "Okay, Mom, I'll bug off."

The following dialogue shows how a sympathetic brief reply prevented futile arguments.

RUTH, AGE EIGHT: Mommy, did you know that junior high school is the school of romance?

MOTHER: Oh?

RUTH: Yes, the boys and girls have parties all the time.

MOTHER: So, you're looking forward to junior high?

RUTH: Oh, yes!

In the past Ruth's mother related she would have lectured her daughter about wasting her time; that school is for learning, not romancing; and that she was altogether too young to think about such things. Long arguments and a spoiled mood would have followed. Instead she acknowledged her daughter's desire.

Often an ounce of humor is worth a ton of words. Twelve-year-old Ron saw his mother unload fresh fruit from the shopping cart, which she usually left on the kitchen counter. With a wry smile he said, "Do something right for once, Mom, and put the fruit in the refrigerator."

"I did something right once. I produced you," his mother replied. "Now help me put the fruit in the refrigerator." Ron started chuckling and helping.

How easy it would have been for Ron's mother to have started a war of words: "What do you mean, Do something right! Who do you think you are to talk to your mother like that?" Instead she expressed her authority with *humor and brevity.*

A father related how delighted he was to hear his child use *humor* to diminish frustration and rage. The day before Christmas he and his eight-year-old daughter, Megan, were trying to put together an artificial Christmas tree. It was not easy to get all the branches to fit and Megan's father grew impatient. At last the tree was ready to be decorated. But as soon as he started to hang a star on one of the branches, the tree collapsed. Her father became furious, shouting: "I've had it!" Megan came over, hugged her father, and said, "Dad, right now, I bet you wish you were Jewish."

Authority Calls for Brevity and for Selective Silence

The following incident illustrates the power of silent authority. Scott, age seven, had hurt his leg, but that did not stop him from going to a Cub Scout party that evening. The next morning he said, "I can't go to school. My leg hurts." His mother was tempted to answer, "If you can go to a party, you can go to school." But she said nothing. The silence was heavy. A few minutes later, Scott asked, "Do you think I should go?" His mother answered, "You're wondering about that." Scott said, "Yes," as he hurried to get dressed.

Scott's mother's silence helped him make his own decision. He, himself, must have come to the conclusion that a leg that is good enough to go to a party is good enough to get him to school. Had his mother pointed this out to him, he would have argued and everyone would have become upset.

Remembering that *less is more* with children, this mother prevented her daughter, Diane, from infecting the rest of the family with her bad mood.

Diane, age twelve, is a vegetarian. As soon as she sat down to dinner one day, she started to complain: "I'm starved. Where's the dinner?"

MOTHER: Hm, you must be very hungry.

DIANE: Oh, eggplant. I don't feel like it.

MOTHER: You're disappointed.

DIANE: There's not enough cheese.

MOTHER: You would like more cheese on your eggplant.

DIANE: Oh, it's okay, I guess. But you usually make it better.

Instead of counter-complaining with "You know I have to prepare special food for you. The least you can do is appreciate it," by reflecting Diane's feelings, her mother avoided an argument.

A Policy on Lying: Learn How Not to Encourage Lying

Parents are enraged when children lie, especially when the lie is obvious and the liar is clumsy. It is infuriating to hear a child insist that she did not touch the paint or eat the chocolate when the evidence is all over her shirt and face.

Provoked lies. Parents should not ask questions that are likely to cause defensive lying. Children resent being interrogated by a parent, especially when they suspect that the answers are already known. They hate questions that are traps, questions that force them to choose between an awkward lie and an embarrassing confession.

Quentin, age seven, broke a new truck given to him by his father. He became frightened and hid the broken pieces in the basement. When his father found the remains of the truck, he fired off a few questions that led to an explosion.

FATHER: Where is your new truck?

QUENTIN: It's somewhere.

FATHER: I didn't see you playing with it.

QUENTIN: I don't know where it is.

FATHER: Find it. I want to see it.

QUENTIN: Maybe someone stole the truck.

FATHER: You are a damned liar! You broke the truck! Don't think you can get away with it. If there's one thing I hate, it's a liar!

This was an unnecessary battle. Instead of sneakingly playing detective and prosecutor, and labeling his son a liar, his father would have been more helpful to his son by stating, "I see your new truck is broken. It did not last long. It's a pity. You really enjoyed playing with it."

The child might have learned some valuable lessons: Dad understands. I can tell him my troubles. I must take better care of his gifts. I have to be more careful.

Thus, it's not a good idea to ask questions to which we already have the answers. For instance, "Did you clean the room as I asked?" while looking at a dirty room. Or, "Did you go to school today?" after having been informed that your daughter did not. A statement is preferable: "I see the room has not been cleaned yet." Or, "We have been told that you skipped school today."

Why do children lie? *Sometimes they lie because they are not allowed to tell the truth.*

Four-year-old Willie stormed into the living room, angry, and complained to his mother: "I hate Grandma!" His mother, horrified, answered, "No, you don't. You love Grandma! In this home we don't hate. Besides, she gives you presents and takes you places. How can you even say such a horrible thing?"

But Willie insisted, "No, I hate her, I hate her. I don't want to see her anymore." His mother, now really upset, decided to use a more drastic educational method. She spanked Willie.

Willie, not wanting to be punished more, changed his tune: "I really love Grandma, Mommy," he said. How did Mommy respond? She hugged and kissed Willie and praised him for being such a good boy.

What did little Willie learn from this exchange? It's dangerous to tell the truth, to share your true feelings with your mother. When you're truthful, you get punished; when you lie, you get love. Truth hurts. Stay away from it. Mommy loves little liars. Mommy likes to hear only pleasant truths. Tell her only what she wants to hear, not how you really feel.

What could Willie's mother have answered if she wanted to teach Willie to tell the truth?

She would have *acknowledged* his upset: "Oh, you no longer love Grandma. Would you like to tell me what Grandma did that made you so angry?" He may have answered, "She brought a present for the baby, not for me."

If we want to teach honesty, then we must be prepared to listen to bitter truths as well as pleasant truths. If children are to grow up honest, they must not be encouraged to lie about their feelings, be they positive, negative, or ambivalent. It is from our reactions to their expressed feelings that children learn whether or not honesty is the best policy.

Lies that tell truths. When punished for truth, children lie in self-defense. They also lie to give themselves in fantasy what they lack in reality. Lies tell truths about fears and hopes. They reveal what one would like to be or do. To a discerning ear, lies reveal what they intend to conceal. *A mature reaction to a lie should reflect understanding of its meaning*, rather than denial of its content or condemnation of its author. *The information gained from the lie can be used to help the child to distinguish between reality and wishful thinking.*

When three-year-old Jasmine informed her grandma that she received a live elephant for Christmas, her grandma reflected her wish rather than tried to prove to her granddaughter that she was a liar. She answered, "You wish you did. You wish you had an elephant! You wish you had your own zoo! You wish you had a jungle full of animals!"

Three-year-old Robert told his father that he saw a man as tall as the Empire State Building. Instead of answering, "What a crazy idea. Nobody is that tall. Don't lie," this father took this opportunity to teach his son some new words while *acknowledging instead of denying his perception*: "Oh, you must have seen a very big man, a gigantic man, an enormous man, a huge man!"

While playing in the sandbox, making a road, four-year-old Craig suddenly looked up, screaming, "My road is getting broken by a storm. What should I do?"

"What storm!" asked Mother in an annoyed tone. "I don't see any storm. So, stop your nonsense."

The storm that Craig's mother ignored in the sandbox broke out in real life. Craig threw a temper tantrum of hurricane proportion. This tempest could have been prevented had the mother recognized and acknowledged her child's perception by entering into his imaginary world, asking, "A storm is washing away the road that you worked so hard to build? Oh . . ." Then, looking up at the sky, she could have added, "Please stop storming up there. You are washing away the road built by my son."

Dealing with Dishonesty:
An Ounce of Prevention Is Worth
a Ton of Investigation

Our policy toward lying is clear: On the one hand, we should not play prosecuting attorney or ask for confessions or make a federal case out of a tall story. On the other hand, we should not hesitate to call a spade a spade. When we find that the child's library book is overdue, we should not *ask*, "Have you returned the book to the library? Are you sure? How come it's still on your desk?" Instead, we should *state*, "I see your library book is overdue."

When the school informs us that our child has failed a math test, we should not ask, "Did you pass your math test? . . . Are you sure? . . . Well, lying won't help you this time! We talked with your teacher and we know that you failed miserably."

Instead, we tell our child directly, "The math teacher told us that you did not pass the test. We are worried and wonder how we can help."

In short, we do not provoke the child into defensive lying, nor do we intentionally set up opportunities for lying. When a child does lie, our reaction should not be hysterical and moralistic, but factual and realistic. *We want our child to learn that there is no need to lie to us.*

Another way parents can prevent children from lying is to avoid the question "Why?" Once upon a time "why" was a term of inquiry. This meaning has long vanished. *It was corrupted by the misuse of "why" as a coin of criticism.* To children "why" stands for parental disapproval, disappointment, and displeasure. It elicits echoes of past blame. Even a simple "Why did you do that?" may suggest "Why in the world did you do something as stupid as that?"

A wise parent avoids harmful questions, such as:

"Why are you so selfish?"
"Why do you forget everything I tell you?"
"Why can't you ever be on time?"
"Why are you so disorganized?"
"Why can't you keep your mouth shut?"

Instead of asking rhetorical questions that cannot be answered, we make statements that show compassion:

"John would be glad if you would share with him."
"Some things are hard to remember."
"I worry when you are late."

"What can you do to organize your work?"
"You have a lot of ideas."

Stealing: Learning the Lessons of Ownership Takes Time and Patience

It is not uncommon for young children to bring home things that do not belong to them. When the "theft" is discovered, it is important to avoid sermons and dramatics. The young child can be guided into the path of righteousness with dignity. He or she is told calmly and firmly: "The toy does not belong to you. It needs to be returned." Or, "I know you wish you could keep the gun, but Jimmy wants it back."

When a child "steals" candy and puts it in his pocket, it is best to confront him unemotionally: "You wish you could keep the candy you put into your left pocket, but it has to be put back on the shelf." If the child denies having the candy, we point and repeat the statement: "I expect you to put the chocolate bar back on the shelf." If he refuses, we take it out of his pocket, saying, "It belongs to the store. It has to stay here."

The wrong question and the right statement. When you are *sure* that your child stole money from your wallet, it is best not to ask, but to tell, about it: "You took a dollar from my wallet. I want it returned." When the money is returned, the child is told: "When you need money, ask me, and we will talk it over." If the child denies the act, we do not argue with him or beg him for a confession; we say, "You know that I know. It has to be returned." If the money has already been spent, the discussion should focus on ways of reimbursement, in chores or by reduction in allowance.

It is important to avoid calling the child a thief and a liar or prophesying an unhappy ending. It is not helpful to ask the child, "Why did you do it?" The child may not know the motivation, and pressure to tell "why" can only result in another lie. It is more helpful to point out that you expect her or him to discuss with you the need for money: "I am disappointed that you did not tell me that you needed a dollar." Or, "When you need money, come and tell me. We'll work something out."

If your child has eaten cookies from the forbidden jar, and there is a mustache of sugar on his or her face, do not ask questions such as "Did anybody take cookies from the jar?" and "Did you by any chance see who took them? Did you eat one? Are you sure?" Such questions usually push the child into making up lies, which adds insult to our injury. The rule is that *when we know the answer, we do not ask the question*. It is better to state openly, for example, "You ate the cookies when I told you not to."

The last statement constitutes adequate and desirable punishment. It leaves the child with discomfort, and the responsibility to do something about the misbehavior.

Teaching Politeness Without Being Rude: Ways to Cultivate Manners

Private models and public manners. Politeness is both a character trait and a social skill; it is acquired through identification with, and imitation of, parents who are themselves polite. Under all conditions, politeness must be taught politely. Yet parents frequently teach it rudely. When a child forgets to say "thank you," parents point it out in front of other people, which is impolite, to say the least. Parents hasten to remind their child to say "good-bye" even before they themselves bid farewell.

Six-year-old Robert has just been handed a wrapped gift. Full of curiosity, he squeezes the box to find out what is in it, as his mother looks on agitated and nervous.

MOTHER: Robert, stop it! You are spoiling the gift! What do you say when you get a present?

ROBERT (*angrily*): Thank you!

MOTHER: That's a good boy.

Robert's mother could have taught this bit of politeness less rudely and more effectively. She could have said, "Thank you, Aunt Patricia, for this lovely gift." It is conceivable that Robert might have followed with his own thank-you. If he had failed to do so, his mother could have dealt with social amenities later when they were by themselves. She could have said, "It was considerate of Aunt Patricia to think of you and get you a gift. Let us write her a thank-you note. She will be glad that we thought of her." While more complicated than a direct reprimand, this approach is more efficient. *The niceties of the art of living cannot be conveyed with a sledgehammer.*

When children interrupt adult conversation, adults usually react angrily: "Don't be rude. It is impolite to interrupt." However, interrupting the interrupter is also impolite. Parents should not be rude in the process of enforcing child politeness. Perhaps it would be better to state, "I would like to finish telling my story."

No good purpose is served by telling children that they are rude. Contrary to hope, it does not steer them into politeness. The danger is that children will accept our evaluation and make it part of their self-image. Once they think of themselves as rude, they will continue to live up to this image. It is only natural for rude children to behave rudely.

Pointed accusations and gloomy prophecies do not help children. Better results are achieved when adults use simple and civil statements. Visits to homes of friends or relatives provide opportunities for demonstrating politeness to children. Visiting should be fun for the parent and child. This can best be achieved when the burden of responsibility for the child's behavior is left to the child and the host.

Children learn that we are reluctant to reprimand them in the homes of others. Trusting geography, they choose these locations to misbehave. This strategy can be counteracted best by letting the hosts set the rules of their own house and carry out their enforcement. When a child jumps on the sofa in Aunt Mary's house, let Aunt Mary decide whether or not the sofa is for jumping, and let her invoke the limit. A child is more likely to obey when restrictions are invoked by outsiders. The mother, relieved of disciplinary obligation, can help the child by voicing understanding of the child's wishes and feelings: "How you wish that Aunt Mary would let you jump on her sofa. You really enjoy doing it, but this is Aunt Mary's home and we have to respect her wishes." If the child counters with "But you let me jump on our sofa," we can respond with "These are Aunt Mary's rules; we have different rules in our home."

This policy can be implemented only when there is agreement between host and guest as to their respective areas of responsibility. Arriving at Aunt Mary's home, Lucy's parent may want to say, "This is your home. Only you know what is and what isn't acceptable behavior here. Please feel free to reprimand my children when you don't like what they are doing." It is the right, and the responsibility, of the hosts to demand compliance with the rules of their home. It is the responsibility of the visiting parent to relinquish temporarily the role of disciplinarian. By appropriate nonintervention, the parent helps the child perceive the reality of the situation.

Summary

Every parent has been perplexed, wondering how to deal with lying, stealing, and the array of misdeeds that litter the growing years. Threats, bribes, promises, sarcasm, and rudeness are not the answer. The most effective solution is to make clear statements that express our values. We do not ask questions to which we already have the answers and, most important, we treat our children with the respect we expect from them. These caring yet authoritative ways of dealing with children's misbehavior also help to strengthen the loving relationship between parent and child.

CHAPTER 4

Responsibility:

Transmitting Values Rather Than Demanding Compliance

Parents everywhere are looking for ways of teaching responsibility to children. In many homes, daily chores are expected to provide the solution to this problem. Emptying trash baskets, preparing meals, mowing lawns, and washing dishes are believed to be effective in making growing children responsible. In actuality, such chores, though important for home management, may have no positive effect on creating a sense of responsibility. On the contrary, in some homes the daily tasks result in daily battles that bring anguish and anger to both children and parents. Forceful insistence on the performance of chores may result in obedience and in cleaner kitchens and yards, but it may have an undesirable influence on the molding of character.

The plain fact is that *responsibility cannot be imposed. It can only grow from within, fed and directed by values absorbed at home and in the community.* Responsibility that is not anchored in positive values can be antisocial and destructive. Gang members often show great loyalty and strong responsibility in relation to one another and to their gang. Terrorists take their duties in dead earnest; they carry out commands, even if they involve sacrificing their own lives.

The Wellspring of Responsibility

While we wish our children to be responsible persons, we want their responsibility to spring from ultimate values, among which are *reverence for life* and *concern for human welfare:* in familiar words, *compassion, commitment, and caring.* We do not usually consider the problem of responsibility in its larger framework. We see responsibility, or the lack of it, in much more concrete terms: in our child's messy room, tardy school attendance, sloppy homework, reluctant piano practice, sulky disobedience, or bad manners.

Yet children may be polite, keep themselves and their rooms clean, do their assignments with precision, and *still make irresponsible decisions.* This is especially true of children who are always told what to do and who therefore have little opportunity to exercise judgment, to make choices, and to develop inner standards.

On the other hand, children who are given the opportunity to make decisions grow up to become psychologically self-supporting, able as adults to choose a mate and work that fulfill them.

Children's inner emotional reaction to our instruction is a decisive element in how much they learn of what we want them to know. Values cannot be taught directly. They are absorbed, and become part of the child, only through identification with, and emulation of, persons who gain his or her love and respect.

Thus, the problem of responsibility in children is referred back to the parent, or more precisely to *the parent's values as expressed in child-rearing practices that enhance loving feelings between parent and child.* The question to consider now is, Are there any definite attitudes and practices that are likely to create a desired sense of responsibility in our children? The rest of the chapter is an attempt to answer this question from a psychological point of view.

Desirable Goals and Daily Practices

Responsibility in children starts with the parents' attitude and skills. The attitudes include a willingness to allow children to feel *all* their feelings; the skills include an ability to demonstrate to children *acceptable ways* of coping with feelings.

The difficulties entailed in meeting these two requirements are most formidable. Our own parents and teachers have not adequately prepared us for dealing with emotions. They themselves did not know how to cope with strong feelings. When confronted with turbulent emotions in children, they tried to deny, disown, suppress, or prettify them. They used phrases that were not helpful:

DENIAL: You don't really mean what you say; you know you love your little brother.

DISOWNING: It's not you; you're just upset by a bad day.

SUPPRESSION: If you mention the word "hate" once more, you'll get the spanking of your life. A nice child does not feel like that.

PRETTIFYING: You don't really hate your sister—maybe you dislike her. In our home we don't hate, we only love.

Such statements ignore the fact that emotions, like rivers, cannot be stopped, only directed. Strong feelings, like the rising waters of the Mississippi, cannot be denied, reasoned with, or talked out of existence. To attempt to ignore them is to invite disaster. They must be recognized and their power acknowledged. They must be treated with respect and diverted with ingenuity. Thus channeled, they may electrify our existence and bring light and joy into our lives.

These are lofty goals. The question still remains: What steps can we take to bridge the gulf between desirable goals and daily practices? Where do we start?

Long-term and Short-term Programs

The answer seems to lie in making a program that is a combination of long-term and short-term efforts. Immediately, we need clear recognition that *character education depends on our relationship with our children and that character traits cannot be transmitted by words but must be conveyed by actions.*

The first step in the long-term program is a determination to become *interested in what children are thinking and feeling, and respond not just to their behavior, their outward compliance or rebellion, but to the feelings that trigger that behavior.*

How can we become aware of what children think and feel? Children give us clues. Their feelings come through in word and in tone, in gesture and in posture. All we need is an ear to listen, an eye to behold, and a heart to feel. *Our inner motto is: Let me understand. Let me show that I understand. Let me show in words that do not criticize or condemn.*

When a child comes home from school silent, slow, and dragging, we can tell by her steps that something unpleasant happened to her. Following our motto, we shall *not* start our conversation with a critical comment, such as:

> *"What kind of face is that?"*
> *"What did you do, lose your best friend?"*
> *"What did you do this time?"*
> *"What trouble are you in today?"*

Since we are interested in how our child feels, we shall *avoid* comments that only create resentment, comments that make her wish she had never come home. *Instead of derision or sarcasm, children are entitled to an empathic response from parents who claim to love them,* such as:

> *"Something unpleasant happened to you."*
> *"It was not a good day for you."*
> *"It seems like you had a hard day."*
> *"Someone gave you a hard time."*

These statements are preferable to such questions as "What's wrong?" "What's the matter with you?" "What happened?" *The questions convey curiosity, the statements convey sympathy.* But even if a parent's sympathetic comments do not immediately change a child's bad mood, the child will absorb the loving feelings the parent's words of understanding convey.

Healing Children's Emotional Wounds

When Daniel told his mother that he had been insulted and pushed around by the school bus driver, it was not her duty to look for the driver's motives or to supply excuses for him. Her task was to respond sympathetically and thus provide emotional first aid with comments such as:

> *"It must have been terribly embarrassing for you."*
> *"You must have been humiliated."*
> *"It must have made you angry."*
> *"You must have really resented him at that moment."*

Such statements would have shown Daniel that his mother understood his anger, hurt, and humiliation, that *she was there for him when he needed her.* Just as parents are quick to provide physical first aid when their children fall and hurt themselves, they also need to learn to provide *emotional first aid* when their children suffer emotional injuries.

There is no escape from the fact that children learn what they live. If they live with criticism, they do not learn responsibility. They learn to condemn themselves and to find fault with others. They learn to doubt their own judgment, to disparage their own ability, and to distrust the intentions of others. And, above all, they learn to live with continual expectation of impending doom.

The easiest way to make children feel that there is something wrong with them is to criticize. It diminishes their image of themselves. Instead of criticism, children need *information without derogation*.

A mother saw her nine-year-old son, Steven, ladling almost the whole pot of chocolate pudding into an over-sized bowl. She was about to rebuke him: "You're so selfish! You only think of yourself! You're not the only one in this house!"

But she had learned that *labeling is disabling*, that pointing out to a child his negative personality attributes does not help him develop into a more caring person. Instead of labeling, she gave information without derogation: "Son, the pudding has to be divided among four people." "Oh, I'm sorry," Steven replied. "I didn't know that. I'll put some back."

Building Relationships with Our Children

Parents who are in the midst of a declared or undeclared war with their children over chores and responsibilities should recognize the fact that this war cannot be won. *Children have more time and energy to resist us than we have to coerce them.* Even if we win a battle and succeed in enforcing our will, they may retaliate by becoming spiritless and moody, or rebellious and delinquent.

Our task then is to build relationships with our children. How do we accomplish this difficult task? By winning them over. This may seem impossible; however, it is merely difficult and we have the capacity to accomplish it once we start to understand their points of view and listen to the feelings that often trigger their misbehavior.

Parents can initiate favorable changes in their child by *listening with sensitivity.*

Children experience frustration and resentment when parents seem uninterested in how they feel and in their point of view.

Example: When Shana's father insisted that she, who was not interested in soccer, accompany the family to watch her kid brother play, she refused. Her father became enraged and threatened to cut off her allowance. Shana stormed out of the house angry, hurt, and feeling unloved. Once her father calmed down, he was able to see her refusal from her point of view and realize that what he wanted to create was a happy family outing but that he had not respected his daughter's feelings. When she returned, he apologized and admitted that it did not make sense for her to join her family at an event that would be unpleasant for her. He also realized that if she had been forced to go, she would have made sure that no one else would enjoy the soccer game, either.

Many parents have an idealized picture of family events and celebrations, ignoring the negative undercurrents that often poison their planned happy occasions. Parents need to choose carefully which family events they insist their children attend. It's not in their best interest to make children feel helpless and resentful and thus suffer the presence of a sullen, angry, and unpleasant child. Why? Because children have many ways to get even with their parents even when it's at their own expense.

Consider this story of Mr. Garret, a bossy man who decided to change his behavior toward his cook, whom he called in, saying,

"From now on I'm going to be nice to you."

"If I'm a little late for lunch, you won't yell at me?"

"No," said his employer.

"If the coffee is not hot enough, you won't throw it in my face?"

"Not anymore!" was his boss' empathic reply.

"If the steak is too well done, you won't deduct it from my salary?"

"No, absolutely not," reiterated Mr. Garret.

"Okay," said the cook, *"then I will no longer spit in your soup."*

There are many ways for children to spit in our soup and make our lives miserable.

Children whose parents do not consider their feelings and point of view may conclude that their ideas are stupid and unworthy of attention and that they are neither lovable nor loved.

Parents who listen with attentiveness and not only hear but also consider their children's strong feelings convey to them *that their opinions and feelings are valued and that they are respected.* Such respect gives the child a sense of self-worth. The feeling of personal worth enables the child to deal more effectively with the world of events and people.

Mirroring Children's Feelings

Have you ever looked into one of those grotesque amusement-park mirrors in which you see yourself exaggerated and contorted? How did it make you feel? Probably uncomfortable. But you laughed because you knew that it was a misrepresentation, that you did not look like that.

But suppose this was the only picture you had of yourself. You could be convinced that this malformed person was the real you. It would not occur to you to distrust the mirror if it was the only image you had of yourself.

Neither do children have any reason to doubt the image their parents mirror to them. They accept even their parents' negative evaluations, which often label them as stupid, lazy, clumsy, inconsiderate, selfish, insensitive, irresponsible, or undesirable. To be told "You look terrible," or "You never do anything right" or "You're so clumsy" does not help a child feel beautiful, capable, or graceful. Many parents label their children stupid, lazy, and a cheat, yet expect such labels to motivate them to change into bright, industrious, and honest people.

Negative parental mirroring can easily distort a child's self-image.

During a television program dealing with children, Ted, age twelve, asked me, "My father calls me lazy, wild, and stupid. Is he right? I don't think I'm like that."

"Tell me, if your father said you were a millionaire, would you believe him?" I inquired.

"No, I know I have only seventeen dollars in the bank, and that's no millionaire. Oh, I see. Just because he says I'm so terrible doesn't mean I am," answered Ted.

"Just as you know how much money you have, you also know the kind of person you are, regardless of what anyone, even your father, may tell you. Because it's your father, whom you love and respect, who called you these names, it only makes it more difficult for you to be sure you are not the person he describes," I reiterated. *Negative labels that might be intended as corrective can burden the recipient for a lifetime.*

Several years ago Pablo Casals, the great cellist and humanist, spoke of children and the importance of making them feel special. He said, "It's not sufficient for children to know that two and two make four. Parents ought to tell their child, 'You are a marvel! You are a miracle! Since the beginning of time, there never was and never will be a child just like you.'"

Some children are lucky. Their parents agree with Pablo Casals and know how to help their children feel special.

Ten-year-old Edith and her mother were shopping in a department store. Suddenly they heard a little boy crying. He seemed to be lost. After a while the security guard found him and helped him look for his mother.

That evening Edith, looking very sad, said to her mother, "I was thinking how terribly frightening it must have been for that little boy when he realized he couldn't find his mother." Her mother's first thought was to reassure her daughter: "Oh, don't worry. They probably found his mother right away." Instead, she decided to take this opportunity to make Edith aware of her caring quality.

MOTHER: Edith, you're really concerned about this lost little boy.

EDITH: I keep thinking how sad he looked.

MOTHER: You showed real empathy and compassion. You seem to sense a child's fear.

EDITH: Gee, Mom, I never thought of myself as anything special.

Preventing "Grapes of Wrath"

Parents should consciously avoid words and comments that create hate and resentment:

> *Insults: You are a disgrace to your school and no credit to your family.*
>
> *Prophesying: The way you act, you will end up in jail!*
>
> *Threats: If you don't settle down, you can forget about your allowance and watching any more TV.*
>
> *Accusations: You are always the first to start trouble.*
>
> *Bossing: Sit down, shut up, and eat your dinner.*

Stating Feelings and Thoughts Without Attacking

In troublesome situations, parents are more effective when they state their own feelings and thoughts *without attacking their child's personality and dignity.* By starting with the pronoun "I," parents can express their angry feelings and describe their child's disapproving behavior without being insulting or demeaning. For example: "I get angry and I'm hurt when my son ignores my repeated request to turn down the volume on his stereo."

When parents listen with sensitivity, work to understand their child's point of view, suspend cutting comments, and reflect their feelings and requirements without insult, a process of change is initiated in the child. The sympathetic atmosphere draws the child nearer to the parents; *their attitudes of fairness, consideration, and civility are noticed and emulated.* These changes will not occur overnight, but the efforts will ultimately be rewarded.

In adopting these attitudes and practices, a parent will accomplish a large part of *educating a child for responsibility*. And yet, example alone is not enough. *A sense of responsibility is attained by each child through his or her own efforts and experience.*

While the parents' example creates the favorable attitude and climate for learning, specific experiences consolidate the learning to make it part of the child's character. Therefore, it is important to give specific responsibilities to children matched to their different levels of maturity.

In most homes children present problems, but parents find the solutions. If children are to mature, they must be given the opportunity to solve their own problems. Here's an example.

Phil's teacher was taking the class on a weekend ski trip. When sixteen-year-old Phil arrived at the bus station, his teacher would not let him join the class on the five-hour trip because he had forgotten his parental permission slip. He was distraught and furious. When he returned home, he confronted his mother: "Mom, if you don't drive me to Vermont, you're going to lose the $100 you paid."

"Phil," she answered, "I know how much you were looking forward to going. I wish I could help you out. But you know how impossible it would be for me to drive you."

"What can I do?" Phil whined.

"Have you considered taking a bus?" his mother suggested.

"No, because I'd have to change too many buses," Phil answered.

"I see you've decided against taking a bus," his mother commented calmly.

For a few minutes longer Phil continued to mumble about how miserable he felt, then he left the room. When he returned, he announced that he'd found a bus that would get him to the mountains without making changes.

As they were driving to the bus station, Phil told his mother how enraged he'd been at his teacher when she said to him, "Well, it isn't our fault that you forgot your permission slip." Then he added, "I was very adult. Do you know how I answered her? 'I'm not interested in finding fault. I'm interested in a solution.'"

"Well," observed his mother, "you know that blaming isn't helpful in a crisis."

This mother's communication skills helped her son to become solution-oriented. As a result, he did not waste time on blaming and shaming. Even though he still would have preferred his mother to bail him out of his difficulties, when encouraged he found a way to get where he wanted to go. By letting Phil find the solution to his problem, his mother helped him feel competent and responsible.

Voice and Choice

Children are not born with a built-in sense of responsibility. Neither do they acquire it automatically at a certain prescribed age. Responsibility, like piano playing, is attained slowly and over many long years. It requires daily practice in exercising judgment and in making choices about matters appropriate to the child's age and comprehension.

Education for responsibility can start very early in the child's life. Responsibility is fostered by allowing children a voice and, wherever indicated, a choice in matters that affect them. *A deliberate distinction is made here between a voice and a choice.* There are matters that fall entirely within the child's realm of responsibility. In such matters the child should have a choice. There are matters affecting the child's welfare that are exclusively within our realm of responsibility. In such matters the child may have a voice, but not a choice. We make the choice, while helping the child accept the inevitable. What is needed is a clear distinction between these two realms of responsibility. Let us examine several areas in which conflicts between parents and children are not uncommon.

Food

Even a two-year-old can be asked whether he wants half a glass of milk or a full glass of milk. (For those parents who are concerned that their child will always choose half a glass, they can start with a larger glass.) A four-year-old can be given a choice between half an apple and a whole apple. And a six-year-old can decide for herself whether she wants her boiled eggs hard or soft.

Children should be deliberately presented with many situations in which they make choices. The parents select the situations; the children make the choices.

A young child is not asked, "What do you want for breakfast?" The child is asked, for example, "Do you want your eggs scrambled or fried?" "Do you want the bread toasted or not?" "Do you want your cereal hot or cold?" "Do you want orange juice or milk?"

What is conveyed to the child is that she has some responsibility for her own affairs. She is not just a recipient of orders, but a participant in decisions that shape her life. From the parents' attitudes, the child should get a clear message: *We provide many options—choosing is your responsibility.*

Eating problems among children are often created by parents who take too great a personal interest in their children's taste buds. They nag children into eating particular vegetables, and tell them (quite unscientifically) which vegetable is most healthful. It's best for the child that the parent not have strong feelings about food; parents offer food of quality and taste and trust children to eat as much or as little as their own appetite demands, provided this does not conflict with medical advice. *Clearly, eating falls within the child's realm of responsibility.*

Not letting children have a voice and, whenever possible, a choice makes it difficult for them to develop a sense of a person who matters, as the following story illustrates. Four-year-old Arthur is sitting in a coffee shop with his mother:

WAITRESS: What will you have?

ARTHUR: I want a hot dog.

MOTHER: Give him a roast beef sandwich!

WAITRESS: What do you want on your hot dog, ketchup or mustard?

ARTHUR (*turning to his mother*): Hey, Mom, she thinks I'm for real!!

Clothes

In buying clothes for small children, it is *our* responsibility to decide what attire they need and what to budget for it. In the store, we select several samples—all acceptable to us in terms of price. The child will choose the one he or she prefers to wear. Thus even a six-year-old can choose her socks, shirts, dresses, pants—from among those her parent has selected. There are many homes in which children get no experience, and develop no skill, in buying clothes for themselves. In fact, there are adults who cannot buy a suit for themselves without having along an adviser to do the choosing.

Older children, particularly, should be allowed to choose even clothes that may be different from the standards acceptable to their parents or to their friends. A child may want to express her individual taste in a way that is uncomfortable for the parent. As long as an older child chooses to use her own money, she should be allowed to buy what pleases her. If her peers make fun of her or make it clear that they find her taste "weird," the chances are she will alter her taste to be more in line with her peers. *The parents can save themselves from criticizing, disapproving, arguing, and creating bad feelings by letting their child's classmates do the work for them.* On the other hand, some children are extremely creative and some parents are comfortable letting those children wear the clothes they like and even design, no matter how different they are from their peers.

There are times when a teen may put on clothes that are very provocative. A parent may invite the teen to consider the message of the clothing: "Do you want to be seen as very unusual?" "Do you want to be seen as sexually available to all who see you?"

Homework

From the first grade on, parents' attitudes should convey that homework is *strictly* the responsibility of the child and the teacher. Parents should not nag children about homework. They should not supervise or check the homework, except at the invitation of the children. (This policy may be contrary to the teacher's wishes.) When parents take over the responsibility for homework, children let them, and parents are never again free of this bondage. Homework may become a weapon in the child's hands to punish, blackmail, and exploit the parents. Much misery could be avoided, and much joy added to home life, if parents would show less interest in the minute details of the child's assignments and instead convey in no uncertain terms, Homework is your responsibility. Homework is for you what work is for us.

There are many fine schools that assign no homework to young children. The students seem to gain just as much wisdom as those who struggle with assignments at the ages of six and seven. The main value of homework is that it gives children the experience of working on their own. To have this value, however, homework must be adjusted to the child's capacity, so that he or she may work independently with little aid from others. *Direct help may only convey to the child that he or she is helpless without parental involvement.* Indirect help, however, may be useful. For instance, we might make sure that the child has privacy, a suitable desk, reference books, and access to a computer. We might also help the child figure out the right time for homework, in accordance with the seasons. In the mild afternoons of spring and fall, a child's fancy will surely turn first to playing and then to homework. In the cold days of winter, homework must come first if there is to be TV later.

Some children like to be near an adult while working at an assignment. They need him or her to listen as they analyze a problem or try to understand a passage in a book. Perhaps it is possible to allow the use of the table in the kitchen or dining room. However, *no comments should be made about manners of sitting, neatness of appearance, or the care of furniture.*

Some children work better when they may chew a pencil, scratch their heads, or rock a chair, or even listen to music. Our comments and restrictions increase frustration and interfere with their mental work. Children resist us less when our requests convey respect and safeguard autonomy.

The child's homework should not be interrupted by questions and errands that can wait. We should remain in the background giving comfort and support rather than instruction and assistance. Occasionally, if invited, we may clarify a point or explain a sentence. However, we should avoid comments such as these: "If you weren't such a scatterbrain, you would remember your assignment." And, "If you only listened to the teacher, you would know your homework."

Our help should be given sparingly but sympathetically. We listen rather than lecture. *We show the road but expect the traveler to reach the destination on his or her own power.*

The following episode illustrates a mother's skill in preventing a problem about homework from becoming an explosion: Helen, age eleven, got up from her desk and challenged her mother: "I don't want to do my homework. I'm too tired."

A common response would have been, "What do you mean, you don't want to do your homework? You're never too tired to play. Only homework makes you tired. See if I care when you come home with a bad report card!"

Instead, Helen's mother replied by *acknowledging* her: "I can see you're tired. You've been working very hard. Come back to your books when you're ready."

A parent's attitude toward the school and the teacher may influence a child's attitude toward homework. If a parent habitually berates the school and belittles the teacher, the child will draw obvious conclusions. Parents should bolster the teacher's position and support policies regarding responsible homework. When the teacher is strict, the parent has a wonderful opportunity to be sympathetic:

> *"It's not an easy year—so much work!"*
> *"It's really tough this year."*
> *"She sure is a strict teacher."*
> *"I hear she demands a lot."*
> *"I hear she is especially tough about homework. I guess there will be lots of work this year."*

It is important to avoid daily flare-ups over homework, such as, "Look here, Amber, from now on you are going to work on your spelling every afternoon of every day—including Saturdays and Sundays. No more playing for you and no TV either." Or "Roger! I am sick and tired of reminding you about homework. Daddy is going to see to it that you focus on your assignments. You will be sorry if you don't."

Threats and nagging are common because they make a parent believe that something is being done about the situation. In reality *such admonitions are worse than useless. They only result in a charged atmosphere, an irritated parent, and an angry child.*

A letter of complaint arrived from school. Ivan, age fourteen, was behind in his studies. His father's first reaction was to call his son and give him a verbal thrashing, and to become punitive: "Listen, Son, from now on you are going to do your homework every day, including weekends and holidays. No movies, no TV, no videogames, and no more visits to friends. I'm personally going to make sure that you get down to business."

This speech had been delivered many times before. It always resulted in a furious father and a defiant son. The increased pressure only increased Ivan's resistance. He became an expert in evasion and concealment.

This time, Ivan's father avoided threats and punishment. Instead he appealed to his son's self-respect. He showed Ivan his teacher's letter and said, "Son, we expect you to do better, to become better informed and more knowledgeable. The world needs capable people. There are still so many problems that need solutions. You could help."

Ivan was so taken by his father's words and tone of voice that he said, "I promise to take my work more seriously."

Many capable children lag in their homework and underachieve in school as an unconscious rebellion against their parents' ambitions. In order to grow up and mature, they need to attain a sense of individuality and separateness from their mother and father. When parents are too emotionally involved with the scholastic record of the child, the child's autonomy is threatened. If homework and high grades become diamonds in the parents' crowns, the child may unconsciously prefer to bring home a crown of weeds that is at least his or her own. By not attaining the parents' goals, the young rebel achieves a sense of independence. Thus the need for individuality and uniqueness may push a child into failure, regardless of parental pressure and punishment. As one child said, "They can take away the TV and the allowance, but they cannot take away my failing grades."

It is apparent that resistance to studying is not a simple problem that can be solved by getting either tough or lenient with children. Increased pressure may increase a child's resistance while a laissez-faire attitude may convey acceptance of immaturity and irresponsibility. The solution is neither easy nor quick. Some children may need psychotherapy to resolve their struggle against their parents and to gain satisfaction in achievement, instead of underachievement.

Others may need tutoring with a psychologically oriented person such as a school counselor or sensitive teacher. *It is imperative that the parent not do the tutoring.* Our goal is to convey to children that they are individuals— apart from us—and responsible for their own successes and failures. When the child is allowed to experience the self as an individual with self-originating needs and goals, that child begins to assume responsibility for his or her own life and its demands.

Allowance: Learning the Meaning of Money

An allowance should not be used as a reward for good behavior or as a payment for chores. It is an educational device that has a distinct purpose: *to provide experience in the use of money by exercising choices and assuming responsibilities.* Therefore, supervision of an allowance would defeat its purpose. What is required is a general policy which stipulates the expenditures that the allowance is expected to cover: treats, lunches, school supplies, et cetera. As the child grows older, the allowance is increased to include additional expenses and responsibilities: club membership dues, the cost of entertainment and clothing accessories, et cetera.

Abuses of an allowance can be expected. Some children will mismanage the budget and spend too much too soon. The abuses should be discussed with the child in a businesslike manner in order to arrive at mutually agreed solutions. In repeated cases of instant spending, it may be necessary to divide the allowance and give it to the child twice or more times a week. The allowance itself should not be used as a club over the child's head to exert pressure for achievement or obedience. It should not be withheld in times of anger, or increased arbitrarily in times of good mood. Even children are uncomfortable with that arrangement, as this anecdote demonstrates:

MOTHER: You have been such a good boy. Here's some money for you to go to the movies.

SON: You don't have to give me any money, Mom. I'll be good for nothing.

What is a fair allowance? There is no universal answer to this question. The allowance should fit our budget. Regardless of neighborhood standards, we should not be pushed into allowing more than we can afford comfortably. If the child protests, we can tell him or her sincerely and sympathetically, "We wish we could give you a larger allowance but our budget is limited." This is a better approach than trying to convince the child that he or she does not really need more money.

Money, like power, can be easily mishandled by the inexperienced. An allowance should not be greater than the child's capacity to manage it. It is better to start with a small allowance, which can be adjusted from time to time, than to overburden the child with too much money. The allowance might be started when the child begins attending school and has learned to count money and make change. One condition is essential to an allowance: The small sum of money left after the fixed expenditures should be the child's own to save or to splurge.

The Care of Pets: A Joint Project in Providing Care

When a child promises to take care of a pet, that child is merely showing good intentions, not proof of ability. A child may need, want, and love a pet, but rarely is he or she able to take care of it properly. The responsibility for the life of an animal cannot be the child's alone. To avoid frustration and recriminations, it is best to assume that a pet for the child means work for the parent. The child may benefit greatly from having a pet to play with and to love. He or she may also benefit from sharing in the care of the pet—but the responsibility for the pet's survival and welfare must remain with the adult. A child may agree to take responsibility for feeding the pet yet still need parents to provide friendly reminders.

Conflict Areas and Realms of Responsibility

Children resist us less when our requests convey respect and safeguard autonomy.

A mother asked her children to clear the table. They procrastinated. She was annoyed. In the past she would yell and threaten. This time she stated facts instead of threats: "When the table is clear, dessert will appear." A flurry of activity told her that she had hit the mark.

Children respond to brief statements that are not phrased as orders. It was a cold, windy day. Todd, age nine, said, "I want to wear my cowboy jacket today." His mother replied, "Check the thermometer. Over forty degrees, cowboy jacket; under forty, winter jacket." Todd checked the thermometer and said, "Oh, well, it's thirty degrees." He put on his winter jacket.

In the past when seven-year-old Amelia and nine-year-old Larry played ball in the living room, their father would yell, "How many times do I have to tell you a living room is not a ball park? There are valuable things here that you can break. You're so irresponsible!" But this time he decided to deal with this recurring situation by giving his children *a choice*: "Kids, you have a choice. One, play outside; or two, give up the game. You decide."

George's mother, who could no longer stand her thirteen-year-old son's long hair, worked out a strategy that preserved his autonomy and dignity. *She gave George a choice*. She said, "Your hair is down to your shoulders. It needs to be trimmed. How it's done is up to you. You can go to the barber or cut it yourself." "You're not getting me to any barber," George answered. "I'll do it myself if I have to."

The next day George brought home a special razor-comb. He asked for his mother's help in making the first crude cut across the back of his hair. Then he spent an hour cutting his hair. When he emerged from the bathroom, he was triumphant: "It looks great, doesn't it?" he glowed.

George's mother related: "I was glad I didn't nag, yell, or force. Instead, I gave my son a choice, which was my way of helping him save face."

Written notes often accomplish what oral comments fail to do.

One parent, tired of nagging, tried humorous ads as a method of recruiting for chores:

WANTED—Young person between the ages of 10 and 12. Must be muscular, intelligent, and daring. Also able to fight off wild animals and cut through dense underbrush between house and garbage can. Applicants please line up at the corner of the dishwasher and kitchen sink.

WANTED—Beautiful princess or prince to help set the banquet table for the royal feast.

The signs brought laughter. What pleased the parent most was the children's attitude. They assumed responsibility without resentment.

Music Lessons: Keeping Harmony at Home

When a child plays a musical instrument, parents will, sooner or later, hear a familiar tune: "I don't want to practice anymore." To face this music with objectivity is not an easy task.

Parents often ask how to motivate children with their music lessons. Here's how one mother accomplished this with *appreciative* questions.

Seven-year-old Ann was playing a piano piece with both hands for the first time.

MOTHER: Did you ever play that piece before?

ANN: No.

MOTHER: You mean this is the first time you're playing it?

ANN: Yes. Did you think I played it before?

MOTHER: Yes.

ANN: My sight-reading sure has improved. Even my teacher noticed it.

MOTHER: It certainly has.

Ann continued playing with enthusiasm. Ann's mother deliberately asked questions that would enhance her daughter's view of her musical ability.

Criticism, on the other hand, kills motivation.

Michael, age ten, has been studying the violin for more than a year. His parents were critical and sarcastic.

They evaluated his progress after each lesson. Whenever he practiced a new piece, slowly and with many mistakes, his father would call out: "Can't you play with fewer mistakes? Don't compose! Follow the notes!" The results were predictable. Michael stopped playing the violin.

To acquire the difficult skill of playing a musical instrument, a child needs *appreciation for effort without criticism for errors*. Mistakes are for correcting, not an excuse for attacking a child's ability.

When a child refuses to go to her music lesson, many parents revert to explanations and threats. Here's a more effective alternative.

MARCIA (*age eight*): I'm not taking violin lessons anymore. The teacher expects me to play every piece perfectly and I can't.

MOTHER: The violin is a difficult instrument. *It isn't easy to play.* Not everyone can take it up. It takes great determination to master it.

MARCIA: Will you stay with me while I practice?

MOTHER: If you want me to.

The mother deliberately did not plead or threaten. She did not tell her daughter what to do: "If you practiced more, you would play better." She appreciated the difficulty of the task and offered token help. This approach seemed to provide Marcia the necessary incentive to continue with her music lessons.

Larry, age ten, had been complaining about his music teacher. His mother did not try to change his mind. Instead, she acknowledged Larry's resentment and offered him choices:

LARRY: My piano teacher expects too much of me. And she talks too much. When I ask a question, she gives me a lecture.

MOTHER: Would you consider taking a vacation from piano lessons, while I try to find another teacher?

LARRY (*shocked*): You want to take away my music lessons? Music is too important to me. I'll never give it up.

MOTHER: Yes, I can hear how much you cherish your music lessons.

LARRY: Maybe this teacher is not that bad. I really learn a lot from her. I think I'll give her another chance.

Larry's mother made it possible for him to change his mind because she did not argue with his complaints. *When parents respect their children's feelings and opinions, they make it possible for them to take their parents' wishes into account.*

SONIA (*age eleven*): I don't want to take any more piano lessons. It's a waste of time and money. I want to take tennis lessons instead.

FATHER: Does it have to be either/or?

SONIA: If I continue with the piano, you'll nag me to practice. I want to avoid a hassle.

FATHER: I'll try not to nag. I'll trust your own schedule of practicing.

Nothing more was said. Sonia started her tennis lessons without giving up her piano lessons.

Some parents, remembering their own enforced music lessons, decide to spare their children such agony. They conclude that to play or not to play is not their question; it is the child's. Children decide whether or not to practice. They play when they feel like it, according to their desire. Except for tuition, which is still the parent's prerogative, *instrument practice is seen as the child's responsibility.*

Other parents, remembering with regret their own overly permissive musical experience, decide that come what may, their child will play. Even before the child is born, her musical medium has already been chosen for her. As soon as she can hold a fiddle, blow a horn, or bang on a piano, she will begin to practice her predestined instrument. The child's tears and tantrums will be disregarded and her resistance overcome. The parents' message is loud and clear: "We pay—you play." Under these conditions a child may or may not achieve musical proficiency. However, the whole enterprise may be too costly. The price is too high if the results include prolonged disturbed relations between parents and child.

The main purpose of music education in childhood is to provide an effective outlet for feelings. A child's life is so full of restrictions, regulations, and frustrations that outlets of release become essential. Music is one of the best avenues of release: *It gives sound to fury, shape to joy, and relief to tension.*

Parents and teachers do not usually look upon music education from this point of view; for the most part they look for skill in reproducing melodies. This approach inevitably involves evaluation and criticism of the child's performance and personality. Too often the results are sadly familiar: The child attempts to give up lessons, avoid the teacher, and terminate the musical "career." In many homes a deserted fiddle, an unused piano, or a mute flute serves only as a painful reminder of frustrated efforts and unfulfilled hopes.

What can parents do? The parents' job is to find a teacher who is kind and considerate—one who knows children as well as music. It is the teacher who holds the key to the child's continuous interest in music and it is the teacher who can open or lock the doors of opportunity. The teacher's vital task is to gain a child's respect and confidence. If the teacher fails in that, he cannot succeed in his instruction: A child does not learn to love music from a teacher whom he or she hates. The teacher's emotional tone has a stronger echo than that teacher's musical instrument.

To prevent avoidable trouble, teacher, parents, and child should discuss—and agree on—several basic rules. The following are examples:

1. No cancellation of a lesson without notification at least one day prior to appointment time.
2. If an appointment must be canceled, the child, not the parent, is the one to call the teacher.
3. Realistic leeway is provided in choosing the time and pace of music practice.

These rules discourage last-minute "mood" cancellations and encourage the child's sense of independence and responsibility. They also convey to the child that, while we have regard for music, we have even greater regard for feelings and ideas.

A child should not be nagged about practicing. No child should be reminded how much the instrument cost and how hard the father, for example, worked for the money. Such statements engender guilt and resentment. They do not create either musical sensitivity or interest.

Parents should refrain from prognosticating about

their child's "great" musical talents. Statements such as the following are very discouraging: "You have marvelous talents, if you only used them." "You can be another Billy Joel, if you would only apply yourself." The child may conclude that the parents' illusions can be best maintained by not putting them to the test. The child's motto may become "If I don't try, I won't disappoint my parents."

A child is encouraged most when he or she knows that difficulties are understood and appreciated. During her third piano lesson, Roslyn, age six, had to try a new skill: to play an eight-note scale with both hands. The teacher demonstrated the exercise with great proficiency, saying, "See, it's easy. Now you try it." Reluctantly and clumsily, Roslyn tried unsuccessfully to imitate her teacher. She returned home from this lesson discouraged.

At practice time, unlike the teacher, her mother said, "It's not easy to play an eight-note scale with one hand. With two hands it is even more difficult." Roslyn agreed readily. At the piano she slowly picked out the right notes with the proper fingers. Mother said, "I can hear the right notes and I can see the right fingers." With obvious satisfaction, her daughter replied, "It is pretty hard." That day Roslyn continued her practicing beyond the agreed time. During the week, she set for herself more difficult tasks and was not satisfied until she learned to play the octave blindfolded. *A child feels more encouraged by sympathetic understanding of difficulties than by advice, praise, or ready-made instant solutions.*

Parent-Teacher Conferences:
Keeping a Focus on Helping the Child

Parent-teacher conferences can be daunting to parents because they often require parents to listen to unpleasant critical comments about their children. How can parents turn the conferences into constructive experiences?

Don's father came to the parent-teacher conference prepared (pad and pen) to record and *translate* any negative comments about his son into positive action.

FATHER: How's Don doing this year?

TEACHER: Well, let me tell you. Your son does not come to school on time. He doesn't do his homework, and his notebooks are messy.

FATHER (*writing*): Oh, you mean Don *needs improvement* in coming to school on time, doing his homework, and keeping his notebooks neat.

When Don's father returned from his conference with the teacher, ten-year-old Don asked, "What did my teacher tell you about me?" His father said, "I wrote down what she said. You may read it if you'd like." Don, who expected familiar remarks about his misbehavior and homework, was surprised when he read his father's notes. Both Don and his father benefited from this note. It helped them to focus on improvements rather than past faults. It avoided blame, it gave direction and hope.

Every parent-teacher conference can end on such a constructive note. Examples:

"Harriet needs improvement in seeing herself as a responsible person worthy of respect and capable of doing her work."

"Frank needs improvement in viewing himself as a person who can contribute to class discussions."

"Celia needs improvement in expressing her anger without insult and in resolving arguments peacefully."

"Bill needs improvement in learning to study independently and completing assignments."

Often, when children change schools, they are asked to repeat the grade they just left. For many parents this is difficult and embarrassing.

When nine-year-old Bob's mother found out that he told his friends that he was going to repeat the fourth grade in his new school, his mother became enraged, screaming, "How do you expect your friends to respect you when you tell them that you have to repeat the fourth grade? Now you see why they don't want to have anything to do with you."

She would have been less destructive had she shared with Bob her embarrassment about his repeating a grade: "I wish it didn't embarrass me that the new school wants you to repeat the fourth grade. I am concerned that your friends will think that you're stupid. But I hope you don't feel the same way. After all, you are repeating the fourth grade only because you're transferring to a more difficult school."

Twelve-year-old Olivia changed schools twice. The first time she transferred from a public school to a private school and was placed in the sixth grade, which she had already completed. But in the next school she was skipped from the eighth grade to the tenth grade. Did that mean that her parents had a stupid daughter in the sixth grade, but a very bright one in the tenth grade? Should they have been ashamed of her the first time and proud of her two years later? Neither would have been helpful. What Olivia needed from her parents was not an evaluation of her intelligence but *their expression of their faith in her ability to cope with the demands of a new school.*

Friends and Playmates: Overseeing Your Child's Social World

Theoretically, we want our children to choose their own friends. We believe in freedom, we oppose coercion, and we know that free association is a basic right in a democracy. However, not infrequently a child brings home "friends" whom we find unacceptable. We may dislike bullies and snobs, or have difficulty tolerating ill-mannered children, but unless their behavior really gnaws at us, it is best to study our child's preferences and attractions before attempting to interfere with his or her choices.

What yardstick can we use to evaluate our child's choice of friends?

Friends should exert a beneficial and corrective influence upon each other. A child needs opportunities to associate with personalities different from, and complementary to, his or her own. Thus a withdrawn child needs the company of more outgoing friends, an overprotected child needs more autonomous playmates, a fearful child should be in the company of more courageous youngsters, an immature child can benefit from the friendship of an older playmate. A child who relies too heavily on fantasy needs the influence of more prosaic children. An aggressive child can be checked by playmates who are strong but not belligerent. Our aim is to encourage corrective relations by exposing children to friends with personalities different from their own.

Some associations need to be discouraged. Infantile children only feed on each other's immaturity. Belligerent children only reinforce each other's aggression. Very withdrawn children do not engage in enough social give-and-take. Delinquent children may reinforce each other's antisocial tendencies. Special care must be taken to prevent children who glamorize criminal behavior from becoming dominant "friends." Because of their greater "experience," they may attain hero status in school or in the neighborhood and serve as undesirable models of identification.

Parents cannot influence their children's friendships unless they have contact with the friends. Parents can invite their children to bring their friends home. They can get acquainted with the friends' parents. They can observe the effects of various friends on their children.

It takes a delicate system of checks and balances to allow children the responsibility of choosing their own friends while we keep the responsibility of ensuring that the choices are beneficial.

Fostering a Child's Independence

A good parent, like a good teacher, is one who makes him- or herself increasingly dispensable to children. The parent finds satisfaction in relationships that lead children to make their own choices and to use their own powers. In conversations with children, *we can consciously use phrases that indicate our belief in their capacity to make wise decisions for themselves.* Thus, when our inner response to a child's request is "yes," we can express it in statements designed to foster the child's independence. Here are a few ways of saying yes:

"If you want to."
"If that is really what you like."
"You decide about that."
"It is really up to you."
"It is entirely your choice."
"Whatever you decide is fine with me."

Our "yes" may be gratifying to the child, but the other statements give the child the additional satisfaction of making his or her own decisions, and of enjoying our faith in him or her.

We all want our children to become responsible adults. The lessons of responsibility go astray unless delivered with respect. Chores, food, homework, allowance, pets, and friendships are some of the areas where parent guidance is important. That guidance must be paired with sensitivity and understanding of their children's struggle toward independence if it is to have the desired effect.

CHAPTER 5

Discipline:

Finding Effective Alternatives to Punishment

Physicians have a motto, *"Primum non nocere,"* which means "Above all, do no damage." *Parents need a similar rule to help them remember that in the process of disciplining their children they do not damage their emotional well-being.*

The essence of discipline is finding effective alternatives to punishment.

Ms. Williams was about to give her first lesson in a school for delinquent boys. She was very apprehensive. As she walked briskly to her desk, she stumbled and fell. The class roared in hilarious laughter. Instead of punishing the students for laughing at her, Ms. Williams rose slowly, straightened up, and said, "This is my first lesson to you: *a person can fall flat on her face and still rise up again."* Silence. The message was received.

Ms. Williams was a true disciplinarian, as all parents can be when they use the force of wisdom rather than threats and punishment to affect children's behavior.

When parents punish children, they enrage them. Suffused with rage and absorbed in grudges, they can't listen or concentrate. In discipline whatever generates rage should therefore be avoided. Anything that enhances self-confidence and respect for one's self and others is to be fostered.

What happens when parents enrage their children? They start to hate themselves and their parents. They want to get even. They become preoccupied with revenge fantasies. When Roger, age seven, was punished and humiliated by his father, he receded into a fantasy world where he became involved with his father's funeral arrangement.

Why do parents enrage children? Not because they're unkind, but unskilled. They are not aware which of their statements are destructive. They are punitive because no one has taught them how to handle a difficult situation without attacking their children.

A mother related the following incident: One day her son, Fred, came home from school, screaming as he opened the door: "I hate my teacher. She yelled at me in front of my friends, she said I disrupt the class with my talking, and then she punished me by making me stand in the hall the whole period. I'm never going back to school!"

Her son's rage unsettled his mother and so she blurted out the first thing that came to her mind: "You know very well that you have to obey the rules. You can't talk whenever you please. And when you don't listen you get punished. I hope you learned your lesson."

After his mother's response to his upset feelings, Fred became enraged at her, too.

If Fred's mother had instead said the following: "How embarrassing to have to stand in the hall! And how humiliating to be yelled at in front of your friends! No wonder you're angry. Nobody likes to be treated that way," her *sympathetic response, which reflected Fred's upset feelings, would have diminished his rage and made him feel understood and loved.*

Some parents may be concerned that, by acknowledging their child's upset and providing emotional first aid, they would send a message that they were not concerned with their child's misbehavior. But as far as Fred's mother was concerned, his disruptive behavior took place in school and his teacher dealt with it. What she felt her suffering son needed from her was not an additional reprimand, but a sympathetic comment and an understanding heart. He needed her help to get over his upset. Empathy, a parent's ability to understand what a child is feeling, is an important and valuable ingredient of child rearing.

Recently in an electronics store, the owner said to me, "I heard you discuss discipline and I don't agree with you." He stretched out the palm of his hand. "This is my psychology," he said proudly.

I asked him whether he applied the same "palm method" in fixing a computer, a stereo, or a TV set. "Oh, no," he replied. "For that you need skill and knowledge. These are complex instruments."

Children, too, need parents who are skilled and knowledgeable, who understand that the "palm method" is as pointless for them as it is for a computer. It fails to achieve its goal. No child says to himself or herself after being punished, "I'm going to improve. I'm going to be more responsible, more cooperative because I want to please this punishing adult."

Discipline, like surgery, requires precision—no random cuts, no careless attacks. The following common absurdity, described by a mother, underscores our challenge: "I have become aware of a personal paradox: I often use tactics similar to those that I try to eradicate in my children. I raise my voice to end noise. I use force to break up fighting. I am rude to a child who is impolite and I berate a child who uses bad language."

Misbehavior and punishment are not opposites that cancel each other; on the contrary, they breed and reinforce each other. Punishment does not deter misconduct. It makes the offender more skillful in escaping detection. *When children are punished they resolve to be more careful, not more obedient or responsible.*

Parents' Uncertainty: The Need for Better Ways

What is the difference between our approach and our earlier generations' approach in disciplining children? What our parents and grandparents did was done with authority; what we do is done with hesitation. Even when in error, they acted confidently. Even when in the right, we seem to act with doubt. Where does our hesitation in relation to children come from? Child psychologists have warned us about the costly consequences of an unhappy childhood, and we are deeply concerned that we may damage our children for life.

The Need to Be Loved

Most parents love their children, but it is important that they not have an urgent need to be loved by them every minute of the day. Those who need children in order to derive justification for their marriage or significance for their lives are at a disadvantage. Afraid of losing their children's love, they dare not deny anything to their children, including control of the home. Sensing their parents' hunger for love, children exploit it mercilessly. They become tyrants ruling over anxious servants.

Many children have learned how to threaten their parents with the withdrawal of love. They use blackmail quite bluntly, saying, "I won't love you if . . ." The tragedy is not in the child's threat, but in the fact that the parents feel threatened. Some parents are really affected by the child's words: They cry and beg the child to continue to love them, and they try to placate the child by being *overly permissive.* This is destructive for both parents and children.

One evening after dinner, fourteen-year-old Jill asked to go to her friend's house to work on a school project. When her father repeated the house rule, "No going out on school nights," Jill argued that the visit wasn't social but involved homework. The father relented and Jill left, promising to be home no later than ten-thirty.

When she did not return by ten-thirty, her father phoned her. "I've decided to stay all night," Jill informed him. He was furious. After an angry exchange, she was ordered home. Jill's father was unaware that by breaking his own rule, he sent his daughter a message that if rules can be broken, so can promises. The next day Jill even bragged to her father: "I can always get you to do what I want. I can talk you into anything."

This incident, a repetition of many others, puzzled her father. He couldn't understand why it was easy for him to make rules, but so difficult to enforce them. He had to agree with Jill that she could talk him into anything. Only when he realized how hurt he was when he felt rejected by Jill, how much he needed to be loved by her, was he able to say "no" and mean it.

Permissiveness and Over-permissiveness

What is permissiveness and what is over-permissiveness? *Permissiveness is an attitude of accepting the childishness of children.* It means accepting that "children will be children," that a clean shirt on a normal child will not stay clean for long, that running rather than walking is the child's normal means of locomotion, that a tree is for climbing, and a mirror is for making faces at.

The essence of permissiveness is the acceptance of children as persons who have a constitutional right to have all kinds of feelings and wishes. The freedom to wish is absolute and unrestricted; all feelings and fantasies, all thoughts and wishes, all dreams and desires, regardless of content, are accepted, respected, and may be permitted expressions through appropriate means. *Fish swim, birds fly, and people feel.* Children cannot help how they feel, but they are responsible for the way they express these feelings. Thus *they cannot be held responsible for their feelings but only for their behavior.* Destructive behavior is not permitted; when it occurs, the parents intervene and redirect it into verbal outlets and other symbolic channels. Permitted symbolic outlets are painting "mean" pictures, running around the block, recording ill wishes on tape, composing caustic poems, writing murder mysteries, et cetera. In short, permissiveness is the acceptance of imaginary and symbolic behavior. *Over-permissiveness is the allowing of undesirable acts. Permissiveness and acceptance of all feelings bring confidence and an increasing capacity to express feelings and thoughts. Over-permissiveness brings anxiety and increasing demands for privileges that cannot be granted.*

Permit Feelings but Limit Acts

The cornerstone of this kind of discipline is the distinction between wishes, feelings, and acts. *We set limits on acts; we do not restrict wishes or feelings.*

Most discipline problems consist of two parts: angry feelings and angry acts. Each part has to be handled differently. Feelings have to be identified and processed; acts may have to be limited and redirected. At times, identification of the child's feelings may in itself be sufficient to clear the air:

MOTHER: It looks as if you are angry today.

RONEN: I sure am!

MOTHER: You feel kind of mean inside.

RONEN: You said it!

MOTHER: You are angry at someone.

RONEN: Yes. You.

MOTHER: Why don't you tell me about it?

RONEN: You didn't take me to the Little League game, but you took Steve.

MOTHER: That made you angry. I bet you said to yourself, "She loves him more than she loves me."

RONEN: Yes.

MOTHER: Sometimes you really feel that way.

RONEN: I sure do.

MOTHER: You know, dear, when you feel that way, come and tell me.

At other times, limits must be set. When Margaret, age four, wanted to cut off her cat's tail "to see what's inside," her father accepted her scientific curiosity, but limited her action in no uncertain terms: "I know you want to see how it looks inside. But the tail has to stay where it is. Let's see if we can find a picture to show you how it looks inside."

When a mother found Ted, age five, doodling on her living-room wall, her first reaction was to pummel him. But he looked so scared that she could not bring herself to hit him. Instead she said: "No, Ted, walls are not for drawing. Paper is. Here are three sheets of paper." And his mother started cleaning up the wall. Ted was so overwhelmed that he said, "I love you, Mommy."

Contrast this to the handling of a similar smearing in another house: "What are you doing? What's the matter with you? Don't you know that you aren't supposed to dirty walls? I just don't know what to do with you."

Helpful and Unhelpful Approaches to Discipline

There is a vast difference between unhelpful and helpful approaches to discipline. In disciplining children, parents sometimes stop undesirable acts, but *ignore the urges that bring about the acts.* The restrictions are set in the midst of angry argument and are often incoherent, inconsistent, and insulting. Furthermore, discipline is administered at a time when children are least able to listen, and in words that are most likely to arouse resistance. More often than not, children are left with the dooming impression that not just their specific acts have been criticized, but that they are *no good as persons*.

In helpful approaches, when we discipline our children we concentrate on helping them with *both their conduct and their feelings*. Parents allow children to speak out about what they feel, but limit and direct undesirable acts. The limits are set in a manner that preserves the self-respect of the parents as well as of the children. The limits are neither arbitrary nor capricious, but educational and character building. The restrictions are applied without violence or excessive anger. Children's resentment of the restrictions is anticipated and understood; *they are not punished additionally for resenting the prohibitions*.

Discipline, thus employed, may lead to voluntary acceptance by children of the need to inhibit and change some behavior. In this sense, parental discipline may eventually lead to *self-discipline*. By identifying with the parents and the values they personify, children attain inner standards for self-regulation.

Three Zones of Discipline: Encouraged, Allowed, and Forbidden

Children need a clear definition of acceptable and unacceptable conduct. They feel more secure when they know the borders of permissible action. We think of children's behavior as falling into three different areas:

The *first* consists of behavior *that is wanted and sanctioned*, the area where our "yes" is given freely and graciously. The *second* includes behavior *that is not sanctioned but is tolerated for specific reasons*. Such reasons may include:

1. *Leeway for learners.* A driver with a learner's permit is not given a ticket when he signals right and turns left. Such mistakes are tolerated for the sake of expected future improvements.

2. *Leeway for hard times.* Special stress situations—accidents, illness, moving into a new neighborhood, separation from friends, death or divorce in the family—call for additional leeway. We grant it because of our appreciation of hard times and new adjustments. We do not pretend that we like this behavior. In fact, our attitudes tell that this conduct is tolerated only because of exceptional circumstances.

The *third* covers conduct that *cannot be tolerated at all and must be stopped.* It includes behavior that endangers the health and welfare of the family or its physical and financial well-being. It also includes behavior forbidden for reason of law, ethics, or social acceptability. *It is as important to be prohibitive in the third area as it is to be permissive in the first.*

One child thought that her father did not have the right standards because he allowed her to hang out late at night. Another boy lost respect for his parents because they did not stop the wild play of his friends who almost demolished his workshop.

Young children have genuine difficulty in coping with their socially unacceptable impulses. The parents must be an ally in the child's struggle for control of such impulses. By setting limits, the parent offers help to the child. Besides stopping dangerous conduct, the limit also conveys a silent message: *You don't have to be afraid of your impulses. I won't let you go too far. It is safe.*

Techniques for Setting Limits

In the setting of limits—as in all education—the product depends on the process. A limit should be so stated that it tells the child clearly (a) *what constitutes unacceptable conduct*; (b) *what substitute will be accepted.* You may not throw dishes; you may throw pillows. Or in less grammatical but more effective English: Dishes are not for throwing; pillows are for throwing. Your brother is not for pushing; your scooter is for pushing. It is preferable that a limit be total rather than partial. There is a clear distinction, for example, between splashing water and not splashing water on your sister. A limit that states, "You may splash her a little, as long as you don't get her too wet," is inviting a deluge of trouble. Such a vague statement leaves the child without a clear basis for making decisions. A limit must be stated firmly, so that it carries only one message to the child: "This prohibition is for real. I mean business." *When parents are not sure of what to do, it is best that they do nothing but think and clarify their own attitudes.* In setting limits, the parent who equivocates is lost in endless arguments. Restrictions, invoked haltingly and clumsily, become a challenge to children and evoke a battle of wills, which no one can win.

A limit must be stated in a manner that is deliberately calculated to minimize resentment, and to save self-respect. The very process of limit-setting, of saying "no," should convey *authority, not insult.* It should deal with a specific event, not with a developmental history. The following is an illustration of an undesirable practice:

Eight-year-old Annie went with her mother to the department store. While her mother shopped, Annie roamed around the toy counter and selected three toys.

When her mother came back, Annie asked confidently, "Which toys can I take home?" The mother, who had just spent too much money on a dress she was not sure she really wanted, blurted out, "More toys? You have more toys than you know what to do with. Everything you see, you want. It's time you learn to curb your appetite."

A minute later, the mother, realizing the source of her sudden anger, tried to placate her daughter and to bribe her with ice cream. But the sorrowful look remained on Annie's face.

When a child requests something that we must deny, we can at least grant her the satisfaction of having the wish for it. *Grant her at least in fantasy what we cannot satisfy in reality.* It is a less hurtful way of saying "no." Thus Annie's mother might have said, "You wish you could take some toys home."

ANNIE: Can I?

MOTHER: What do you think?

ANNIE: I guess not! Why not? I really want a toy!

MOTHER: But you can have a balloon or some ice cream. You choose which you would rather have.

Perhaps Annie would make her choice. Or perhaps Annie would cry. In either case, the mother would stick to her decision, and to the offered choices. She may again show her understanding by mirroring her daughter's desire for toys—but the limit would be upheld: "You wish you could have at least one of the toys. You want it very much. Your crying tells me how much you want that toy. How I wish I could afford to buy it for you today."

When a daughter announces that she doesn't want to go to school, instead of insisting, "You have to go to school. Every child has to go to school. It's the law. I don't want any truant officer coming to our house," a more caring response would at least *grant the wish in fantasy*: "How you wish you didn't have to go to school today. You wish instead of Monday it would be Saturday and you could go and play with your friends. You wish you could at least sleep some more. I know. What would you like for breakfast?"

Why is granting in fantasy less hurtful than flat denial? Because the parent's detailed response shows that she understands how her daughter *feels*. When we are understood, we feel loved. How would you feel if you were admiring an expensive beautiful dress in the window of an elegant boutique and your beloved looked at you and said, "What is the matter with you?! What are you looking at! You know we have financial problems. There is no way we'll ever be able to afford something expensive like that." Your beloved's remarks are unlikely to generate loving feelings. They would only make you feel angry and depressed.

But what if he had acknowledged your wish and said, "Oh, honey, how I wish we could afford that beautiful dress. I can see it on you with the right jewelry and a velvet cape. How beautiful you would look. I would be so proud to be your escort at even the most glamorous party."

Neither response, unfortunately, gets you the dress. But the second response at least does not inflict hurt, does not cause resentment, and is, thus, more likely to strengthen loving feelings.

Many years ago I visited an elementary school in an Inuit village in Alaska where I entertained the children by playing the harmonica. When I finished, a child came up to me and said, "I want your harmonica." I could have answered, "No, I can't give you the harmonica. It's the only one I have, and I need it. Besides, my brother gave it to me." The child would have felt rejected and the happy, festive mood would have been ruined. Instead I granted in fantasy what I could not give in reality by saying, "How I wish I had a harmonica to give you!" Another child then came up with the same request and so I answered, "How I wish I had two harmonicas to give away." Eventually, all twenty-six children came up and I just added the numbers, ending with "How I wish I had twenty-six harmonicas, one for each of you." It became a game that the children seemed to enjoy.

After I described this incident in my newspaper column, a magazine editor wrote, "Now when I have to reject an article, I start with 'How we wish we could publish your article.'"

Different Ways of Phrasing Specific Limits

There are ways to express limits that stir resistance and other ways that invite cooperation, as follows:

1. The parent *recognizes the child's wish and puts it in simple words:* "You wish you could go to the movies tonight."
2. The parent *states clearly the limits on a specific act:* "But the rule in our house is 'no movies on school nights.'"
3. The parent *points out ways in which the wish can be at least partially fulfilled:* "You may go to the movies on Friday or Saturday night."
4. The parent *helps the child to express some of the resentment* that is likely to arise when restrictions are imposed, and then sympathizes:

"It is obvious that you don't like the rule."
"You wish there weren't such a rule."
"You wish the rule said, 'Every night is movie night.'"
"When you grow up and have your own home, you're sure going to change this rule."

It's not always necessary or feasible to phrase the limit in this pattern. At times, it's necessary to state the limit first and mirror feelings later. When a child is about to throw a stone at his sister, the mother should say, "Not at her, at a tree!" She will do well to deflect the child by pointing in the direction of the tree. She can then get at the feelings and suggest some harmless ways of expressing them:

"You may be as angry as you want at your sister."
"You may be furious. Inside yourself, you may hate her, but there will be no hurting."
"If you want to, you may throw stones at the tree."
"If you want to, you may tell or show me how angry you are."

Limits should be phrased in a language that does not challenge the child's self-respect. *Limits are heeded better when stated succinctly and impersonally.* "No movies on school nights" arouses less resentment than "You know you can't go to the movies on school nights." "It's bedtime" is more readily accepted than "You are too young to stay up that late. Go to bed." "Time is up for TV today" is better than "You have watched enough TV today, turn off the set." "No shouting at each other" is obeyed more willingly than "You better stop shouting at him."

Limits are accepted more willingly when they point out the function of an object: "The chair is for sitting, not for standing" is better than "Don't stand on the chair." "The blocks are for playing, not for throwing" is better than either "Don't throw blocks" or "I am sorry I can't let you throw blocks; it is too dangerous."

Children Need Healthy Outlets for Their Energy

Many discipline problems with young children arise over restraint of physical activities. For example:

"Don't run—can't you walk like a normal child?"

"Don't jump all over."

"Sit up straight."

"Why must you stand on one foot when you know you have two feet?"

"You'll fall and break a leg."

Children's motor activities should not be over-restrained. For the sake of both mental and physical health, children need to run, jump, climb, skip, et cetera. Concern for the health of the furniture is understandable, but it must not supersede concern for the health of the children. Inhibition of physical activity in young children results in emotional tension, which may be expressed in aggression.

Arranging a suitable environment for direct discharge of energy in muscular activities is a prime—but frequently overlooked—condition for good discipline in children and for an easier life for parents. Children need active play. There are many opportunities for children's physical activities: playing ball, jumping rope, running, swimming, ice-skating, playing baseball, doing gymnastics, Roller-blading, bicycling. Schools have become more aware of the need for children to be physically active and thus offer organized sports during and after school and a serious physical education program.

Clear Enforcement of Discipline

When a parent's feelings about a restriction are crystal clear and the restriction is phrased in inoffensive language, a child will usually conform. Yet, from time to time, a child will break a rule. The question is, What is to be done when a child transgresses a stated restriction? The educational process requires that the parent adhere to the role of a kindly but firm adult. In reacting to a child who violates a limit, the parent must *not become argumentative and verbose.* The parent must not be drawn into a discussion about the fairness or unfairness of the limit. Neither should the mom or dad give a long explanation for it. It is unnecessary to explain to a child why he must not hit his sister, beyond saying that "people are not for hurting," or why she must not break the window, beyond saying that "windows are not for breaking."

When a child exceeds a limit, the child's anxiety mounts because he or she expects retaliation and punishment. The parent does not need to increase the child's anxiety at this time. *If parents talk too much, they convey weakness*—at a time when they must convey strength. It is at times like this that the child needs an adult ally to help control impulses without loss of face. The following example illustrates an unhelpful approach to limits:

MOTHER: I see that you won't be satisfied until you hear me yelling. Okay. [*Loudly and shrilly*] Stop it—or you'll be sorry! If you throw one more thing, I'll do something drastic!

Instead of using threats and promises, this mother could have expressed her very real anger more effectively:

"It makes me mad to see that!"
"It makes me angry!"
"I feel furious!"
"These things are not for throwing! The ball is for throwing!"

In enforcing a limit, a parent must be careful not to initiate a battle of wills. In this example, five-year-old Margaret and her father are enjoying an afternoon in the park:

MARGARET (*at the playground*): I like it here. I am not going home now. I am going to stay another hour.
FATHER: You say you are, but I say you are not.

Such a statement may lead to one of two results, both of them undesirable: defeat for the child or defeat for the father. A better approach is to *focus on the child's desire* to stay in the playground, rather than on her threat to defy authority. For instance, the father could have said, "I see that you like it here. I suppose you wish you could stay much longer, even ten hours. It's time to go home."

If, after a minute or two, Margaret is still persistent, her father may take her by the hand or pick her up and lead her out of the playground. With young children, action frequently speaks louder than words.

Parents Are Not for Hitting

Children should never be allowed to hit their parents. Such physical attacks are harmful for both children and parents. It makes children feel anxious and afraid of retaliation. It makes parents feel angry and hateful. The prohibition against hitting is necessary to spare children guilt and anxiety and to enable the parents to remain emotionally hospitable to their children.

From time to time, one witnesses degrading scenes in which a parent, to escape, say, from being kicked in the shin, suggests to the child that he hit her on the hand instead. "You may hit me a little, but you mustn't really hurt me," begged a thirty-year-old mother of a four-year-old child, stretching her arm out in his direction. One is tempted to intervene and say, "Don't do it, lady. It is harmful to the child to let him strike his parent." The mother should have stopped the child's attack immediately: "No hitting. I can never let you do that." Or "If you are angry, tell it to me in words."

The limit against hitting a parent should not be modified under any circumstances. Effective upbringing is based on mutual respect between parent and child *without the parent's abdicating the adult role*. In telling a child to "hit but not hurt," the mother is asking a small child to make too fine a distinction. The child is irresistibly challenged to test out the prohibition and to find out the difference between hitting playfully and hurting seriously.

Children Are Not for Hitting

Spanking, though in bad repute, is still practiced by some parents. It is usually applied to child rearing as a last resort after the more conventional weapons of threats and reasoning have failed. Frequently, it is not planned, but occurs in a burst of anger when parents have reached the end of their endurance. For the moment, spanking seems to work: It relieves pent-up tension in the parent and makes the child obey at least for a while. And, as some parents say, "It clears the air."

If spanking is so effective, why do we have such uneasy feelings about it? Somehow we cannot silence our inner doubts about the long-term effects of physical punishment. We are a little embarrassed by the use of force and we keep saying to ourselves, "There ought to be a better way of solving problems."

What if you lose your temper and hit a child? Most parents do sometime. "There are times when I get so furious with my son, I feel like murder," one mother said. "When my choice is between killing and smacking, I smack. When I calm down, I tell my son, 'I'm only human. I can take that much and no more. I hit you. But it's against my values. When I'm pushed beyond the brink of my endurance, I do things I don't like. So don't push me.'"

Hitting children should be as unacceptable as car accidents are. Yet car accidents do happen. But a driver's license does not give advance permission for car accidents. It does not state, "You're sure to have some car accidents, so don't drive carefully." On the contrary, we are admonished to drive carefully. Neither should hitting children be a prescribed method for disciplining them, even though accidental hitting cannot always be avoided.

It's almost impossible to bring up children without hitting them from time to time. But we don't have to plan for it. We should not consider physical punishment as a response to our children's provocation or our own irritation. Why not? Because of the lesson it demonstrates. It teaches children undesirable methods of dealing with frustration. It dramatically tells them, "When you're angry or frustrated, don't look for solutions. Hit. That's what your parents do." Instead of displaying our ingenuity by finding civilized outlets for savage feelings, we give our children not only a taste of the jungle but also permission to hit.

Most parents get upset when they witness their older children hitting their younger siblings, unaware that when they spank their small children they give the older children permission to do the same.

A six-foot father saw his eight-year-old son hit his four-year-old sister. He became enraged and started spanking his son while admonishing him: "This will teach you not to hit anyone smaller than you." One evening seven-year-old Jill and her father were watching television. Jill was sucking her fingers, emitting disconcerting sounds. Her father was annoyed and said, "Please, stop. I find your sucking noises disturbing." Nothing happened. He repeated his request. Still, nothing happened. After the fourth time, he became furious and hit Jill. She started to cry and hit her father. This made her father even angrier: "How dare you hit your father!" he shouted. "Go to your room immediately." When she refused, he carried her upstairs. She continued to cry while the television blared and no one watched.

Jill could not understand why it was permissible for a big man to hit a *little* girl but forbidden for her to hit someone *bigger* than she. This episode left her with the distinct impression that you can only hit someone smaller and get away with it.

Jill's father could have used a more effective way of winning his daughter's cooperation than hitting. Instead of waiting until he could no longer control his anger, he could have said to his daughter, "Jill, *you have a choice*: You can stay here and stop sucking your fingers or you can leave the room and continue to enjoy sucking your fingers. You decide."

One of the worst side effects of physical punishment is that it may interfere with the development of a child's conscience. *Spanking relieves guilt too easily*: The child, having paid for the misbehavior, feels free to repeat it. Children develop what may be called a bookkeeping approach to misconduct: It permits them to misbehave and thus go into debt on one side of the ledger and pay off in weekly or monthly spanking installments. Periodically, they provoke a spanking by egging on their parents. Sometimes they just ask for punishment or punish themselves.

Marcy, age four, was brought for consultation. She was pulling her hair out in her sleep. Her mother revealed that when she became angry at her daughter, she would threaten, "I am so mad at you that I feel like pulling out all your hair." Marcy, who must have felt that she was bad enough to deserve such cruel punishment, obliged her mother in her sleep.

A child who asks for punishment needs help with managing guilt and anger, not compliance with the request. This is not an easy task: In some situations, guilt and anger can be reduced by discussing the misdeeds openly. *When the child is given better ways of expressing guilt and anger, and when parents learn better ways of setting and enforcing limits, the need for physical punishment is diminished*.

By showing sympathetic understanding for our children's many feelings, we prepare them to become emotionally intelligent. By respectfully setting and enforcing limits on their unacceptable acts, we prepare them to honor the rules of the social world.

CHAPTER 6

Positive Parenting:

A Day in a Child's Life

Civilization has cast parents in the role of naysayers who must say "no" to many of the small child's greatest pleasures: no sucking of the thumb, no touching of the penis, no picking of the nose, no playing in dirt, and no making of noise. To infants, civilization is cold and cruel: Instead of a soft breast, it offers a hard cup; instead of instant relief and warm diapers, it offers a cold pot and the demand for self-restraint.

Some restrictions are inevitable if the child is to become a social being. However, parents should not overplay their role of police for civilization, lest they invite avoidable resentment, resistance, and hostility.

Getting Off to a Good Start

Parents should not be the ones to wake up their school-age children every morning. Children resent parents who disturb their sleep and disrupt their dreams. They dread parents coming into their rooms, pulling off their blankets, and cheerfully singing, "Rise and shine." It is better for all concerned if children are awakened by an alarm clock, rather than by what must look to them like an "alarm mother" or "alarm father."

Emily, age eight, had difficulty getting out of bed in the morning. Every day she tried to stay in bed for a few endless minutes more. Her mother was sometimes sweet and sometimes sour, but Emily was always persistent: slow to rise, unpleasant at breakfast, and late to school. The daily arguments left her mother tired and resentful.

The situation improved dramatically when the mother gave her daughter an unexpected gift—an alarm clock. In the gift box Emily found a note: "To Emily, who does not like other people to wake her too early in the morning. Now you can be your own boss. Love, Mother." Emily was surprised and delighted. She said, "How did you know that I don't like anyone to wake me up?" Her mother smiled and said, "I figured it out." When the alarm clock rang the next morning, she said to Emily, "It's so early, honey. Why don't you sleep another few minutes?" Emily jumped out of bed saying, "No. I'll be late for school."

A child who cannot wake up easily should not be called lazy; and the child who does not rise and shine instantly should not be labeled grumpy. *Children who find it hard to be alert and zestful in the morning do not need ridicule.* Rather than engage them in a battle, it is best to let them enjoy another ten golden minutes of sleep or daydreams. This can be accomplished by setting the alarm clock to ring earlier. Our statements should convey empathy and understanding:

> *"It is hard to get up this morning."*
> *"It is such a pleasure to lie in bed and dream."*
> *"Take another five minutes."*

Such statements make the morning bright; they create a climate of warmth and intimacy. In contrast, the following statements of anger or scorn invite cold and stormy weather:

> *"Get up, you lazy thing!"*
> *"You get out of that bed this minute."*
> *"My God, you are another Rip Van Winkle."*

Or concern over their health: "Why are you still in bed? Are you sick? Does anything hurt? Do you have a tummy ache? A headache? Let me see your tongue." All this suggests to the child that the way to receive tender care is to be sick. Children may also think that parents will be disappointed if they deny having any of the maladies that were so graciously listed. Children may feel obliged to pretend that they feel sick.

The Tyranny of Timetables: The Rush Hour

When children are hurried, they take their time. Most often they resist adults' "Hurry up!" by engaging in a slow-down. What appears as inefficiency is in reality children's very efficient weapon against the tyranny of timetables that are not theirs.

Rarely should children be told to rush. Instead, they should be given *realistic time limits,* and left with the challenge to be ready on time:

> *"The school bus will be here in ten minutes."*
>
> *"The movies start at one o'clock. It is twelve-thirty now."*
>
> *"Dinner will be served at seven o'clock. It is six-thirty now."*
>
> *"Your friend will be here in fifteen minutes."*

The intent of our brief statement is to convey to the children that we expect, and take it for granted, that they will be on time. Sometimes positive prospects can help. We might offer, for example, "As soon as you are ready for school, you may watch cartoons until we leave for school."

Breakfast: Meals Without Morals

Breakfast is not a good time for teaching children universal philosophies, moral principles, or polite manners. It is an appropriate time for parents to prepare nourishing meals while helping them get out on time for school.

In general, breakfast is a difficult part of the day. Often the parents or the children are sleepy and grouchy, and arguments may easily degenerate into recriminations and accusations, as this example illustrates:

DEBBIE (*rummaging through the refrigerator, discarding one item after another*): What's for breakfast? There's never anything to eat in this house, you never buy me anything I *like!*

MOTHER: (*upset and defensive*): What do you mean I never buy you anything you like? I buy you everything you like—it's you who can't decide what to eat. Now I want you to sit down and eat what's in front of you and then you can go to school!

Debbie's behavior made her mother angry; she then reciprocated by making her daughter even angrier, and everyone left for work and school in a bad mood.

It's important not to let a child decide the parent's response or mood. Instead of counter-attacking, Debbie's mother could have *acknowledged* her complaint and thus preserved a pleasant morning.

MOTHER: You don't seem to find anything you like this morning.

DEBBIE: No, there's nothing I like. I'm really not very hungry. I'll just have a banana.

Another mother related: "In the past, small incidents became traumatic events for me and my children. The proverbial molehill became a mountain several times each day. But now I have learned to understand my children's messages and respond to them sympathetically, as I did a few days ago at the breakfast table when my five-year-old daughter, Ramona, refused to eat breakfast and complained."

RAMONA: My teeth are tired. They feel very sleepy on the bottom.

Instead of ridiculing her, her mother *acknowledged* her complaint.

MOTHER: Oh, your lower teeth are not yet awake.
RAMONA: No, and this one tooth is having a bad dream.
MOTHER: Let me see. Oh, honey, it's loose.
RAMONA: Will it fall into my cereal?

When her mother reassured her that it was not that loose yet, Ramona's spirits lifted and she picked up her spoon and started to eat her cereal.

Stan's father shared the following: "My first reaction to any mishap is an overreaction that sets the mood for further conflict. Then I try to put out the fire I myself started, like a clever man who knows how to get out of a hole that a wise man would never have gotten into in the first place. Recently, I have decided to behave like a wise man rather than a clever one. Instead of blaming when my children get into trouble, I offer help, as I did recently. My son, Paul, age ten, likes to prepare his own breakfast. One morning I heard him whimpering in the kitchen. He was poaching two eggs, and one of them splattered on the floor. Instead of screaming 'Look what you've done! What a mess! Why can't you be more careful?' I said, 'You got up quietly, you made such beautiful eggs for yourself, and one fell down just like that.'"

PAUL (*meekly*): Yes.
FATHER: And you are hungry.
PAUL (*looking brighter*): But there's one egg left on the plate.
FATHER: While you're eating one egg, I'll poach you another one.

Complaints: Dealing with Disappointment

Parents are continually confronted with children's complaints, which usually make them angry. In order not to escalate the anger and get into an argument by counter-complaining or being defensive, *they need to learn to respond to complaints by acknowledging the child's complaint.* For example:

SELMA: You never buy me anything.

MOTHER: There's something you would like me to buy you. *Not:* How can you say that after all the beautiful clothes I bought you only last week? You never appreciate anything I do for you. That's your trouble!

JULIAN: You never take me anywhere.

FATHER: Where would you like to go? *Not:* How can I, when you always end up making a scene?

ZACHARY: You're always late.

MOTHER: You didn't like waiting for me. *Not:* And you're never late? You don't want to remember every time I waited for you.

JESSICA: You don't care what happens to me.

FATHER: You wish I had been there when you fell; when you needed me. *Not:* How can you say that after all I have sacrificed to make you happy?

"Never" and "always" are favorite words of children. They live in a world of extremes. But parents who have learned that gray is more common than black and white can teach their children by restraining themselves from using those expressions.

Getting Dressed: The Battle of the Shoestring

In some homes parents and children are entangled in a daily battle of the shoestring. Says one father, "When I see my son with shoes unlaced, I am fit to be tied. I want to know if we should force him to tie the laces, or just let him walk around sloppy. Happy as he may be, shouldn't we teach him responsibility?" It is best not to tie up the teaching of responsibility with the tying of shoes; it is better to avoid arguments by buying the child a pair of slip-on sneakers or by tying a small child's laces without comment. One can rest assured that *sooner or later the child will learn to keep his shoes tied, unless his peers do otherwise.*

Children should not go to school dressed in their most expensive clothes. They should not have to worry about keeping clothes clean. The child's freedom to run, jump, or play ball should take precedence over neatness of appearance. When the child returns from school with a dirty shirt, a parent might say, "You look like you had a busy day. If you want to change, there is another shirt in the closet." It's not helpful to tell the child how sloppy she is, how dirty she looks, and how sick and tired we are of washing and ironing her shirts. *A realistic approach does not rely on a child's capacity to put cleanliness ahead of playfulness.* Instead, it accepts that children's clothes will not stay clean for long. A dozen inexpensive wash-and-wear shirts contribute more to mental health than do twelve sermons on cleanliness.

Going to School: Helping Is Better Than Haranguing

It can be expected that in the morning rush, a child may forget to pick up books, glasses, lunch box, or lunch money. It is best to hand the child the missing item without adding any sermons about forgetfulness and irresponsibility.

"Here are your glasses" is more helpful to the child than "I want to live to see the day when you remember to wear your glasses." "Here is your lunch money" is more appreciated by the child than the sarcastic question "And what will you buy your lunch with?"

The child should not be given a list of admonitions and warnings before leaving for school. "Have a pleasant day" is a better parting phrase than the general warning "Don't get into trouble." "I'll see you at two o'clock" is more instructive to the child than "Don't go wandering off in the streets after school."

The Return from School: Providing a Warm Welcome

It's desirable that a parent or other caring adult be home to greet children upon their return from school. Rather than asking questions that bring worn-out answers— "How was school?" and "Okay" or "What did you do today?" and "Nothing"—a parent can *make statements that convey an understanding of the trials and tribulations at school*:

"You look as though you had a hard day."
"I bet you could not wait for school to end."
"You seem glad to be home."

In most situations making statements is preferable to asking questions.

With a large number of single-parent families and mothers who work, many children no longer find a parent at home to personally greet them. But leaving a written or e-mailed message of affection can mitigate the parent's absence. Some parents of school-age children use letters and notes to deepen the relationship with their children. It is easier for them to express appreciation and love in writing. Some parents leave messages on a tape recorder or on videotape. The child can listen to parents' words over and over again. Such messages encourage meaningful communication between parent and child and lessen the loneliness that children feel when coming from school to enter an empty home.

Homecoming: Reconnecting at the End of the Day

When working parents return home in the evening, they need a quiet transition period between the demands of the world and the demands of the family. Neither the mother nor father should be met at the door with a bombardment of complaints and requests or with a flood of requisitions and recriminations. A "no questions" period helps create an oasis of tranquillity that adds greatly to the quality of family life. From early childhood, children need to learn that when harried parents come home from work, they need a short period of calm and comfort. Dinner, on the other hand, should be conversation time. *The stress should be less on food and more on food for thought.* There should be few remarks on how and what the child eats, *few disciplinary actions,* and many examples of the old-fashioned art of conversation.

Some parents take turns taking one of the children to a restaurant of his or her choice to have some private one-on-one time. While eating a hamburger or pizza, the child, having the mother's or father's full attention, can share concerns with the parent.

Bedtime: War or Peace

In many homes bedtime is bedlam time, with the children and parents forming a mutual frustration society. Children try to stay up as late as possible, while the mother and father want them asleep as soon as possible. The evenings become prime nagging time for parents and tactical evasion time for children.

Preschool children need the mother or father to tuck them in. *Bedtime can be utilized for intimate conversation with each child.* Children then begin to look forward to bedtime. They like having "time alone together" with their mother or father. If the parent takes pains to listen, the child will learn to share his fears, hopes, and wishes. These intimate contacts relieve children of anxiety and lull them into pleasant sleep.

Some older children also like to be tucked in. Their wish should be respected and fulfilled. They should not be ridiculed or criticized for wanting what looks to parents like "baby stuff." Bedtime for older children should be flexible: "Bedtime is between eight and nine [or nine and ten]. You decide when you want to go to bed." The range of times is determined by parents. The specific time within that range is determined by the child.

It is best not to get involved in a fight when a child claims that he "forgot" to go to the bathroom or that she wants a glass of water. However, a child who keeps calling parents back to the room should be told, "I know you wish I could be with you longer. But now is Mom and Dad's time to be together." Or "It would be nice if I could visit with you longer but now is my time to get ready for bed."

Parental Prerogative:
No Entertainment License Required

In some homes, children have the power of veto over their parents' comings and goings. Parents have to get permission from several children for an evening away from home. Some parents shun going to the movies or to the theater because of the expected battle at home.

Parents do not need permission or agreement from children on how to live their lives. If a child cries because his mother and father are going out in the evening, the fears need not be condemned, but such wishes need not be complied with. We can understand and sympathize with the desire not to be left with a babysitter, but it is not necessary to buy an entertainment license from the child. To the weepy child we say with empathy, "I know you wish we were not going out tonight. Sometimes when we are not here, you get scared. You wish we would stay with you, but your mother and I are going to enjoy a movie [or friends, or dinner, or a dance] tonight."

The content of the child's objections, pleadings, or threats can be ignored. Our reply should be firm and friendly: "You wish I could stay with you, but this is my time to go out."

Television: The Naked and the Dead

No discussion of a child's day would be complete without estimating the influence of television on values and conduct. Children like to watch TV and play games on their computers. Many prefer these activities to reading books, listening to music, or engaging in conversation. For advertisers, children are a perfect audience: They are suggestible and believe the commercials. They learn idiotic jingles with amazing facility and are only too happy to pester their parents with silly slogans. And they ask so little of the programs: No originality is required and no art is necessary. Furry or plastic heroes hold their interest. So, for hours on end, day after day, children are confronted with violence and murder intermingled with jingles and advertisements.

Parents feel two ways about television. They like the fact that it keeps the children occupied and out of trouble, but they are concerned about possible harm to the children.

Television can encourage violence, trivialize relationships, support stereotypes, and undermine prosocial behavior. Further, television consumes a significant part of a child's day. More of the child's time is spent with the TV set than with either their father or mother. *Even if spectacles of sex and brutality were nothing more than innocent fun, they do keep children from more constructive activities*. As one prominent psychologist has observed, people simply do not have those optimal experiences called flow while watching television. The best condition for growth is when "a person's skills are fully involved in overcoming a challenge that is just about manageable" (Csikszentmihalyi, 1998, p. 30). For children, that might mean writing poems or short stories, making a sculpture from clay, or building a castle with blocks. It might entail enacting dramas with siblings or adventures with a friend. Growth and satisfaction are more likely to come from focused effort than from witless watching.

In some homes children are allowed to view TV only one hour a day. In other homes they are allowed certain times and programs, selected with the parents' approval. These parents believe that television, like medication, must be taken at prescribed times and in the right doses.

Two distinguished pediatricians have made a specific recommendation: "In the first three years, no more than one half hour per day should be spent watching TV. After age three, an additional half hour of TV or computer time could be shared with a parent" (Brazelton and Greenspan, 2000, p. 49).

An increasing number of parents feel that the choice of programs cannot be left entirely to children. They are not willing to let questionable characters influence their children in their own home. Parents who want to protect their children from exposure to daily doses of sordid sex and vivid violence can now install a "parental monitoring system" on their TV and computer. While children need not be sheltered from all tragedy, they should be protected from entertainment in which human brutality is not a tragedy, but a formula.

It is not enough for parents to oversee the quantity and nature of children's media consumption. Parents can open the doors for children to learn, connect, and contribute through healthy relationships, happy play, and satisfying hobbies.

CHAPTER 7

Jealousy:

The Tragic Tradition

Jealousy between siblings has an ancient and tragic tradition. The first murder recorded in the Old Testament was Cain's slaying of his brother, Abel. The motive was sibling rivalry. Jacob escaped death at the hands of his brother, Esau, only by leaving home and hiding in a foreign land. And Jacob's sons were so envious of their younger brother, Joseph, that they threw him into a pit before changing his death sentence to life slavery and selling him to a passing caravan in the desert.

What does the Bible tell us about the nature and origin of jealousy? In each of these cases, jealousy was sparked by a parental figure who showed favoritism toward one of the children. Cain slew his brother after God favored Abel's gift, but not his. Esau became jealous because his mother showed preferential treatment for Jacob by helping him receive his father's blessings. And Joseph was envied by his brothers because their father loved him best; he gave him a "coat of many colors" and did not discipline him when he indulged in impudent boasting.

These biblical stories of envy and revenge show that jealousy has been an issue for parents and children since ancient times. However, now we can learn how to minimize feelings of jealousy in our children.

The Not-So-Blessed Event: It Feels Like an Intrusion to Siblings

In contrast to their parents, children do not question the existence of jealousy in the family. They have long known its meaning and impact. Regardless of how thoroughly they were prepared, the arrival of a new baby brought jealousy and hurt. No explanation can gracefully prepare a prima donna for sharing the spotlight with a rising newcomer. *Jealousy, envy, and rivalry will inevitably be there.* To fail to anticipate them, or to be shocked at their appearance, is an ignorance that is far from bliss.

The coming of a second baby is a first-rate crisis in the life of a young child, whose space orbits have suddenly changed and who needs help in orientation and navigation. To be of help rather than to be merely sentimental, we need to know the child's true sentiments.

In announcing the blessed event to a young child, it is best to avoid long explanations and false expectations, such as, "We love you so much and you are so very wonderful that Daddy and Mommy decided to have another baby just like you. You'll love the new baby. It will be your baby, too. You'll be proud of the baby. And you'll always have someone to play with."

This explanation sounds neither honest nor convincing. It is more logical for the child to conclude, "If they really loved me, they wouldn't look for another child. I'm not good enough, so they want to exchange me for a newer model."

How would any wife feel if her husband came home one day and announced, "Honey, I love you so much and you are so wonderful that I have decided to bring another woman to live with us. She'll help you with the housework and you'll no longer be lonesome while I'm at work. After all, I have more than enough love for two women." I don't think she would be ecstatic about such an arrangement. She would wonder why she is not enough and why he would think that she would look forward to sharing him with another woman. It's more likely that she would feel jealous and unloved.

It hurts to share a parent's or a spouse's love. In a child's experience, sharing means getting less, like sharing an apple or a piece of gum. The prospect of sharing a parent is worrisome enough, but our expectation that the child should delight in the newcomer is beyond logic. As pregnancy proceeds, suspicions seem more valid. The child notices that even though the baby has not yet arrived, it has already occupied the parents. The mother is less available. She may be sick in bed, or tired and resting. The anxious child cannot even sit in her lap, because it is taken by a hidden, yet ever present, intruder. The father is more involved with the mother and less available for play or other activities.

Homecoming: Introducing the Intruder

The coming of a baby can be announced without pomp and fanfare to a young child. It is sufficient to state, "We are going to have a new baby in our family." Regardless of children's immediate reactions, we will know that there are many unasked questions on their minds and many unexpressed worries in their hearts. Fortunately, as parents, we are in a good position to help our children live through these times of crisis. *Nothing can change the fact that a new baby is a threat to a child's security.* For a firstborn it's also a threat to his uniqueness. It's especially painful for a firstborn child whose experience has not included sharing his parents. As the only apple in his parents' eyes, he can't be too happy when the arrival of the new baby spells the end of his sojourn in the Garden of Eden.

However, whether a child's character will be enhanced or warped by the stress and strain of the crisis depends on our wisdom and skill.

The following example illustrates a helpful introduction to a future sibling.

When Virginia, age five, found out that her mother was pregnant, she reacted with great joy. She painted a picture of sunshine and roses about life with a brother. The mother did not encourage this one-sided view of life. Instead she said, "Sometimes he will be fun, but sometimes he will be trouble. Sometimes he will cry and be a nuisance to all of us. He'll wet the crib and mess in his diapers. I will have to wash him, feed him, and take care of him. You may feel left out. You may feel jealous. You may even say to yourself, 'She does not love me anymore—she loves the *baby.*' When you feel that way, be sure to come and tell me, and I'll give you extra loving, so you won't have to worry. You'll know that I love you."

Some parents hesitate to use such an approach. They fear putting "dangerous" ideas into a child's head. These parents can be assured that such ideas are not new to the child. Our statement reflects understanding of feelings. It immunizes against guilt and it invites intimacy and communication. A child is bound to feel anger and resentment for the new baby. *It is best that the child feel free to voice anguish to us openly, rather than languish silently.*

Expressing Jealousy: Words Are Better Than Symptoms

The following incident illustrates how one mother helped three-year-old Jordan express his upset feelings about the arrival of the new baby. The baby was expected in three weeks. One day Jordan burst into tears:

JORDAN: I don't want the new baby in the house. I don't want you and Daddy to play with him and to love him.

MOTHER: You're upset about the new baby. You wish there would be no new baby.

JORDAN: Yeah, I just want Mommy, Daddy, and Jordan.

MOTHER: You get angry, just thinking of the new baby.

JORDAN: Yeah, he'll take away all my toys.

MOTHER: You're even a little scared.

JORDAN: Yeah.

MOTHER: You're saying to yourself, Mommy and Daddy won't love me as much and won't have as much time for me.

JORDAN: Yeah.

MOTHER: Well, Jordan, remember you'll always be the only Jordan we have and that makes you very special. And the love we feel for you we'll never feel for anyone else.

JORDAN: Not even the baby?

MOTHER: Not even the baby can take away our love for Jordan. Honey, anytime you feel sad and angry, you come and tell me and I'll give you some special loving.

After the baby arrived, Jordan expressed his resentment by squeezing him, yanking his feet, being very rough with him. Mother admonished him: "The baby is not for hurting but you can draw a picture of him and then cut the picture into pieces, if you wish."

When children repress their jealousy, it comes out in disguised ways in symptoms and misbehavior. Thus when children resent their siblings, but are forbidden to voice their feelings, they may dream that they pushed the younger ones out of tenth-floor windows, for example. The dreamers may become so frightened that they may wake up screaming. They may even run to the siblings' beds to check if they are still there. They may be so delighted to find them in one piece that the parents may mistake relief for love. Nightmares are the child's way of telling in pictures what they fear to tell in words. It is better for children to express jealousy and anger in words rather than in terrifying dreams.

Soon after the birth of a sister, Warren, age five, had a sudden series of wheezing attacks. His parents thought that Warren was very protective of his sister and that "he loved her to death" (perhaps "to death" was an apt description). The physician could find no physical basis for Warren's asthma and he referred him to a mental health clinic, where he might learn to express jealousy and anger in words rather than in wheezes. Some children express their jealousy in coughing and skin rashes, not in words. Others wet the bed, thus expressing with one organ what they should be able to express with another. Some children become destructive: They break things instead of voicing their resentments. Some children bite their nails or pluck their hair as a cover-up for wanting to bite and hurt their brothers and sisters. All these children need to express their feelings in words rather than in symptoms. *Parents are in a key position to help children unlock their feelings.*

The Many Faces of Jealousy

To be on the safe side, parents need to assume that jealousy exists in their own children, even though it is not visible to the untrained eye. Jealousy has many faces and many disguises: It can manifest itself in constant competitiveness or in avoidance of all contests, in pushy popularity or in wallflower meekness, in reckless generosity or in ruthless greed. The bitter fruits of unresolved childhood rivalries are all around us in adult life. They can be seen in the irrational rivalry of the person who is in a perpetual race with every car on the road, or who cannot gracefully lose a tennis game, or who is always ready to bet life and fortune in order to prove a point, or who needs to contribute more than others even when it is more than can be afforded. They can also be seen in the person who shuns all competition, who feels defeated before a struggle begins, who is always ready to take a backseat, who does not stand up even for legitimate rights. Thus sibling rivalry affects a child's life more than most parents realize. It may indelibly stamp personality and distort character. It can become the theme of a troubled life.

The Origins of Jealousy

Jealousy originates in an infant's desire to be the parents' only "dearly beloved." This desire is so possessive that it tolerates no rivals. When brothers and sisters arrive, the child competes with them for the *exclusive* love of both parents. The competition may be open or hidden, depending on the parents' attitudes toward jealousy. Some parents are so angered by sibling rivalry that they punish any overt sign of it. Other parents bend backward almost acrobatically to avoid giving cause for jealousy. They try to convince their children that all of them are loved equally and therefore have no reason to be jealous. Gifts, praise, vacations, favors, clothes, and food are measured and doled out with equality and justice for all. Yet neither of these approaches brings relief from envy. *Neither equal punishment nor equal praise can quench the desire for exclusive love.* Since such a desire is unfulfillable, jealousy can never be totally prevented. However, whether the fire of jealousy will flicker safely or flare up dangerously depends on our attitudes and acts.

Dealing with Jealousy: Words and Attitudes That Make a Difference

Under normal conditions, age and sex differences may cause jealousy among siblings. The older brother is envied because he has more privileges and greater independence. The baby is envied because she is more protected. A girl envies her brother because he seems to have greater freedom. A boy envies his sister because she seems to receive special attention. Danger develops when parents, out of their own needs, give sex differences preferential emphasis.

The preferred child often becomes the victim when parents, as in this story, shower affection and gifts on her. These parents were not only obvious in their preference for a long-awaited girl after the birth of several boys, but they also insisted that the older boys assume responsibility for their sister. Blaming their sister for receiving special privileges, rather than their parents for favoring her, the boys made her life miserable. Unfortunately, her brothers' unresolved jealousy not only poisoned their childhood but also deprived them of a loving sibling relationship in adulthood.

When the parents prefer the helplessness of a baby to the independence of a six-year-old, or vice versa, jealousy will be intensified. The same is true if a child is overvalued because of gender, looks, intelligence, musical abilities, or social skills. *Superior natural endowment may cause envy, but it is the parental overprizing of a trait or a talent that leads to relentless rivalry among children.*

It is not suggested that older and younger children should be treated alike. On the contrary, age should bring new privileges and new responsibilities. An older child will have, as a matter of course, a larger allowance, later bedtime hours, and more freedom to stay out with friends than a younger child. These privileges are granted openly and graciously so that all children will look forward to growing up.

The younger child may envy the privilege of the older one. We can help that child deal with feelings, not by explaining facts, but by understanding emotions:

"You wish you too could stay up late."
"You wish you were older."

"You wish you were not six years old, but nine years old."
"I know, but your bedtime is now."

Parents may also unwittingly foster jealousy by demanding that one child make sacrifices for another: "The baby needs your crib." "Sorry. We cannot get your new skates this year. What with the new baby, we need the extra money."

The danger is that the child may feel deprived not merely of possessions but also of affection. Therefore, such demands should be cushioned with affection and appreciation.

Words of Compassion: Moving Past Jealousy

The very young express their jealousy undiplomatically: They inquire whether babies ever die, suggest that "it" be sent back to the hospital or put in the trash. The more enterprising youngsters may even engage in military operations against the invader. They may harass the child mercilessly: They may hug boa-constrictor style and may push, punch, or pummel whenever possible. In extreme cases, a jealous sibling can cause irreversible harm.

As parents, we cannot allow a child to bully his brother or sister. Sadistic attacks, whether physical or verbal, must be stopped because they harm both the victim and the bully. And both children need our strength and care. Fortunately, *to protect the physical safety of the young child, we do not need to attack the emotional security of the older child.*

When a three-year-old child is caught harassing the baby, the child should be stopped promptly and the motives stated openly:

"You don't like the baby."
"You are angry at him."
"Show me how angry you are. I'll watch."

The child should be handed a large doll or paper and markers. The child may lecture the doll or draw angry lines. We do not suggest to the child what to do. Our role is to observe with a neutral eye and to respond with a sympathetic tongue: We will not be shocked by the ferocity of feelings. The feelings are honest and the attack is harmless. It is better that the anger be vented symbolically against an inanimate object than directly against a living baby or symptomatically against him- or herself. Our comments should be brief:

"You are showing me how angry you are!"
"Now Mommy knows."
"When you get angry, come and tell me."

This approach is more helpful in reducing jealousy than either punishment or insult. In contrast, the following approach is unhelpful. When a mother caught her son, Walter, age four, dragging his baby brother by his feet, she exploded: "What is the matter with you? You want to kill him? You want to kill your own brother? Don't you know that you can maim him for life? You want him to be a cripple? How many times have I told you not to take him out of his crib? Don't touch him, just don't touch him, ever!" Such a reaction will intensify Walter's resentment. What would be helpful? "Babies are not for hurting. Here's your doll, honey. You can drag it all you want."

Older children, too, should be faced with their feelings of jealousy. With them it is possible to converse more openly:

"It's easy to see that you don't like the baby."

"You wish he were not here."

"You wish you were the only one."

"You wish you had me all to yourself."

"You get angry when you see me fuss with her."

"You want me to be with you."

"You were so angry that you punched the baby. I cannot ever allow you to hurt her, but you can tell me when you feel left out."

"When you feel all alone, I will make more time for you, so that you won't feel lonely inside."

Quality or Equality: Love Uniquely, Not Uniformly

Those parents who want to be absolutely fair to each child often end up being furious with all their children. Nothing is so self-defeating as measured fairness. When a mother cannot give a bigger apple or a stronger hug to one child for fear of antagonizing the other, life becomes unbearable. The effort entailed in measuring either emotional or material giving can make any person tired and angry. Children do not yearn for equal shares of love: *They need to be loved uniquely, not uniformly.* The emphasis is on quality, not equality.

We do not love all our children the same way, and there is no need to pretend that we do. We love each child uniquely, and we do not have to labor so hard to cover it up. The more vigilant we are in preventing apparent discrimination, the more alert each child becomes in detecting instances of inequality.

Unwittingly and unwillingly, we find ourselves on the defensive against the child's universal battle cry, "No fair."

Let us not be taken in by the children's propaganda. Let us neither claim extenuating circumstances, nor proclaim our innocence, nor disprove their charge. Let us resist the temptation to explain the situation or to defend our position. Let us not be drawn into endless arguments about the fairness or unfairness of our decisions. And above all, let us not be pushed into rationing or portioning our love for the sake of fairness.

To each child, let us convey the uniqueness of our relationship, not its fairness or sameness. When we spend a few moments or a few hours with one of our children, *let us be with that child fully.* For that period, let the boy feel that he is our only son and let the girl feel that she is our only daughter. When we are out with one child, let us not be preoccupied with the others; let us not talk about them or buy them presents. For the moment to be memorable, our attention must be undivided.

When a child's desire for our undivided love is acknowledged, the child is reassured. When that desire is understood and compassionately appreciated, the child is comforted. When each child is valued in his or her uniqueness, the child is strengthened.

Divorce and Remarriage: Another Arena of Jealousy

Another form of jealousy can surface for children of divorced parents, which may be experienced by a child who enjoys a close attachment with the custodial parent.

All seems to go well until that close relationship is threatened by an intruder, in this case an adult who takes an interest in the child's parent.

It is not unusual for children to feel insecure after one of the parents leaves home. They reason, "If one parent can abandon me, so can the other." As a result they become very protective of the parent with whom they are left. They watch the parent's every move to make sure that he or she does not form an attachment with another adult. They make it difficult for the parent to date, throwing tantrums when she or he speaks on the phone and being as obnoxious as possible when the date visits. They are even willing to give up sleepovers in order to watch over their parent. The last thing they want is to share their parent with a strange adult.

What is a mother or father to do?

They need to understand their children's predicament, empathize with troubled feelings, and encourage them to voice their concerns by reflecting and acknowledging their feelings:

> "This is a difficult time for you. I'm asking you to make another adjustment. First, you had to get used to not having Daddy [or Mommy] living with us and living alone with me. And now you are asked to reorganize your life so that it will include a stranger who is not your parent."
>
> "You're worried that if I fall in love, I will no longer love you."
>
> "You don't want anyone to come between us."
>
> "You're wondering if I would leave you and go away with this person."

"You wish I wouldn't need anyone but you to love me."

"You don't want to share me with this stranger."

"You wish he would go away and our life would continue as it was."

It's the parent's love and understanding that can mitigate children's fears and help them to adjust to their parent's new adult love.

CHAPTER 8

Some Sources of Anxiety in Children:

Providing Emotional Safety

Parents are aware that every child has a full share of fear and anxiety. They are not aware, however, of the sources of such anxiety. Parents frequently ask, "Why is my child so fearful?" One father went so far as to say to his anxious child, "Stop this utter nonsense. You know you have nothing to be afraid of!"

It may be helpful to describe some of the sources of anxiety in children and to offer some ways of coping with anxiety.

Anxiety Due to Fear of Abandonment: Reassuring Through Preparation

A child's greatest fear is of being unloved and abandoned by parents. As John Steinbeck put it so dramatically in *East of Eden:* "The greatest terror a child can have is that he is not loved, and rejection is the hell he fears. . . . And with rejection comes anger, and with anger some kind of crime in revenge. . . . One child, refused the love he craves, kicks the cat and hides his secret guilt: and another steals so that money will make him loved; and a third conquers the world—and always the guilt and revenge and more guilt."

A child should never be threatened with abandonment. Neither in jest nor in anger should a child be warned that he or she will be deserted. One occasionally overhears an exasperated parent in the street or supermarket scream at a dawdling child, "If you don't come right away, I'll leave you here." Such a statement will arouse the ever-lurking fear of abandonment. It fans the flames of the fantasy of being left alone in the world. When a child dawdles beyond toleration, it is better to drag that child by the hand than to threaten with words.

Some children feel frightened if a parent or caregiver is not home when they return from school. Their dormant anxiety of being abandoned is momentarily awakened. As already suggested, it is helpful to leave a message as to parents' whereabouts on the bulletin board, via e-mail, or by means of a tape recorder. The taped messages are especially helpful for young children. The parents' calm voice and loving words enable them to bear temporary partings without excessive anxiety.

When the tides of life force us to be separated from our young children, separation must be preceded by preparation. Some parents find it hard to convey that they will be away for an operation, a vacation, or a social obligation. Fearing their child's reaction, they sneak out at night or when the child is in school and leave a relative or a sitter to explain the situation.

A mother of three-year-old twins had to undergo surgery. The atmosphere at home was tense and troubled, but the children were told nothing. On the morning of hospitalization, the mother, with a shopping bag in hand, pretended that she was going to the supermarket. She left the house and did not return for three weeks.

The children seemed to wilt during this time. The father's explanations were no consolation. They cried themselves to sleep every night. During the day, they spent much time at the window, fretting for their mother.

Children take the stress of separation more easily if they have been prepared for the experience beforehand. Meaningful preparation requires much more than ordinary verbal explanation. It requires communication in the child's native language of toys and play, a language that talks to the child's heart.

In another case, two weeks before entering the hospital, a mother told her daughter Yvette, age three, about the pending event. Yvette showed little interest, but her mother was not fooled by the lack of curiosity. She said, "Let's play Mother Is Going to the Hospital." She produced a set of dolls (bought for this occasion or made with the child's help), which depicted the family figures, a doctor, and a nurse. While manipulating the appropriate dolls and speaking for them, the mother said, "Mommy is going to the hospital to get well. Mommy will not be home. Yvette wonders, Where is Mommy? Where is Mommy? But Mommy is not home. She is not in the kitchen, not in the bedroom, not in the living room. Mommy is in the hospital, to see a doctor, to get well. Yvette cries, I want my mommy. I want my mommy. But Mommy is in the *hospital* to get well. Mommy loves Yvette, and misses her. She misses her every day. She thinks about Yvette and loves her. Yvette misses Mommy, too. Then Mommy comes home and Yvette is so happy to hug and kiss her mommy."

The drama of separation and reunion was played out by the mother and daughter over and over again. At first her mother did most of the talking, but soon Yvette took over. Using the appropriate dolls, she told the doctor and nurse to take good care of Mommy, to make her well, and to send her home soon.

Before her mother left, Yvette asked her to repeat the play once more. Yvette supplied most of the lines and ended her performance reassuringly: "Don't worry, Mommy, I'll be here when you come back."

Before leaving, her mother made several other helpful arrangements: She acquainted Yvette with the new nanny, she put a large photograph of herself and Yvette on the dresser, and on a cassette she recorded several of Yvette's favorite stories for her to listen to before going to sleep as well as a loving message. During moments of inevitable loneliness, her mother's picture and spoken words reassured Yvette of the nearness of her mother's love.

Anxiety Due to Guilt: A Little Goes a Long Way

Wittingly and unwittingly parents arouse guilt in children. Guilt, like salt, is a useful ingredient in flavoring life, but it must never become the main course. When a child has transgressed a rule of social or moral behavior, there is a place for disapproval and guilt. However, when a child is forbidden to have negative feelings or "nasty" thoughts, that child will inevitably have too much guilt and anxiety.

To prevent unnecessary guilt, parents should deal with children's transgressions the way a good mechanic deals with a car that breaks down. He does not shame the owner; he points out what has to be repaired. *He doesn't blame the car's sounds or rattles or squeaks; he uses them for diagnostic purposes.* He asks himself, What is the probable source of the trouble?

It is a great comfort for children to know inwardly that they are really free to think as they please without being in danger of losing their parents' love and approval. When there is a disagreement, statements such as the following are helpful: "You feel one way, but I feel another way. We feel differently on the subject." "Your opinion seems true to you. My opinion is different. I respect your view, but I have another view." Unwittingly, parents may create guilt in children by being wordy and giving unnecessary explanations. *This is especially true of parents who believe they must govern by consent even when the subject is intricate and the child immature.*

Five-year-old Zachary was angry with his nursery school teacher because she had been out sick for two weeks. On the day of her return, he grabbed her hat and ran out into the yard. Both his mother and teacher followed him.

TEACHER: The hat belongs to me and it needs to be returned.

MOTHER: Zachary, you know perfectly well that the hat is not yours. If you keep the hat, Miss Marta may catch a cold and be sick again. She was sick, you know, for two weeks. Now, Zachary, you don't want your teacher to be sick again. Do you?

The danger is that such an explanation may make Zachary feel responsible for, and guilty about, the teacher's sickness. The long explanation was irrelevant and harmful. All that was necessary at that moment was to retrieve the hat. *A hat in the hand is better than two explanations in the yard.*

Perhaps later the teacher will discuss with Zachary his anger about her absence, and point out better ways of coping with it.

Anxiety Due to Mistrust or Impatience: Giving a Child Room to Grow

When a child is prevented from engaging in activities and assuming responsibilities for which he or she is ready, the inner reaction is that of resentment and anger. Little children do not quickly master skills with polished proficiency. They take a long time to tie their shoes, to button their coats, to put on their jackets, to unscrew the lid of a jar, or to turn a doorknob. *The best help that can be offered to them is tolerant waiting and a light comment about the difficulty of the task.* "It is not easy to put on a jacket." "The lid of that jar is hard to unscrew."

Such comments are helpful to the child whether failing or succeeding in the efforts. If the child succeeds, there is the satisfaction of knowing that a difficult chore was conquered. *If the child fails, there is the consolation that his parents knew the task was hard.* In either case, the child experiences sympathy and support, which leads to greater intimacy between parent and child. Failure at a task does not have to make the child feel inadequate. *It is essential that a child's life not be ruled by the adult's need for efficiency.* Efficiency is the enemy of infancy. It is too costly in terms of the child's emotional economy. *It drains the child's resources, prevents growth, stifles interests, and may lead to emotional meltdowns.* Children need opportunities to experiment, struggle, and learn without being rushed or insulted.

Anxiety Due to Friction Between Parents: The Civil War with Uncivil Consequences

When parents fight, children feel anxious and guilty—anxious because their home is threatened, guilty because of their actual or imagined role in the family friction. Justifiably or not, children often assume that they are the cause of domestic strife. Children do not remain neutral in the civil war waged by their parents. They side either with their father or mother. The consequences are harmful to character development. When parents are forced to compete for their children's affection, they frequently use means such as bribery, flattery, and lies. The children grow up with divided loyalties and abiding ambivalence. Furthermore, the need to protect one parent from the other and the opportunity to play one parent against the other leave a mark on children's characters. From early childhood, they become aware of their inflated worth to the bidding rivals, and they put an ever-increasing price on themselves. They learn to manipulate and exploit, to plot and blackmail, to spy and gossip. They learn to live in a world where integrity is a liability and honesty a hindrance.

Parents may manage their differences in calm discussion or save them for private time. While it is helpful for children to know that parents have differences that require negotiation, it is not helpful for children to witness their parents attacking each other.

This situation is exacerbated when parents divorce and the children are used as pawns in the ongoing battle between them. Often they are asked to spy on the other parent, encouraged to complain about that parent and to show a preference. They are also used as a conduit for transmitting unpleasant messages. When that happens, life certainly does not improve for the children. Often children have to assume the adult role by reassuring their parents that they love both of them.

For children of divorced parents, life is problematic enough without being subjected to the continued unpleasantness that led to the divorce. They need to be reassured that they are loved by both parents and that they will not be involved in their parents' squabbles. *After a divorce, children also need time to mourn the loss of their secure home and to get adjusted to their new reality.*

Anxiety Due to Life's End: An Enigma Veiled in Mystery

To adults, the tragedy of death lies in its irreversibility. Death, so final and eternal, is the end of all hope. Therefore death is personally inconceivable; we cannot imagine our own cessation, the dissolution of our own selves. The self consists of memories and hopes, of a past and a future, and people cannot see themselves without a future. The consolation that faith brings belongs precisely in this realm. It offers people a future, so they may live and die in peace.

If death is a riddle to adults, to children it is an enigma veiled in mystery. Young children cannot comprehend that death is permanent; that neither parents nor prayers can bring back the departed. The futility of magic wishes in the face of death is a severe blow to children. It shakes their belief in their power to influence events by wishful thinking, and it makes them feel weak and anxious. What children see is that, in spite of tears and protests, a beloved pet or person is no longer around. Consequently they feel abandoned and unloved. Their fear is reflected in the question often asked of parents: "After you die, will you still love me?"

Some parents try to protect their children from the experience of pain and grief inherent in the loss of someone they loved. If a goldfish or turtle dies, they hurry to replace it with a new one, hoping that the child will not notice the difference. If a cat or dog dies, they rush to offer the grieving child a prettier and costlier substitute. What lessons do children learn from these early experiences of sudden loss and quick replacement? They may conclude that the loss of loved ones is of no great importance, that love may easily be transferred and loyalty easily shifted.

Children (and adults) should not be deprived of their right to grieve and to mourn. They should be free to feel sorrow in the loss of someone loved. Children's humanity is deepened, and their character ennobled, when they can lament the end of life and love. The basic premise is that children should not be excluded from sharing the sorrows as well as the joys that inevitably arise in the course of family life. When a death occurs and the child is not told what happened, he or she may remain shrouded in nameless anxiety. Or the child may fill the gap in knowledge with fearful and confused explanations. They may blame themselves for the loss and feel separated not only from the dead but also from the living.

The first step in helping children face their loss is *to allow them to express fully their fears, fantasies, and feelings.* Comfort and consolation come from sharing deep emotions with a listener who cares. The parents may also put into words some of the feelings that a child is bound to have, but may find difficult to express. For example, after the death of a grandmother to whom the child was attached, a parent might say:

"You miss Grandma."
"You miss her a lot."
"You loved her so much. And she loved you."
"You wish she were with us."
"You wish she were still alive."
"It is hard to believe that she died."
"It is hard to believe that she is no longer with us."
"You remember her so well."
"You wish you could visit her again."

Such statements convey to children the parent's interest in their feelings and thoughts, and encourage them to share their fears and fantasies. They may want to know whether dying hurts, whether the dead ever come back, whether they and their parents will ever die. The answers should be brief and truthful: When one dies, the body feels no pain; a dead person does not return; all people eventually die.

In talking to children about death, it is best to avoid euphemisms. When told that her grandfather went to his eternal sleep, one four-year-old girl asked if he took his pajamas with him. She was also afraid that Grandpa was angry at her because she had not said good night to him before he went to sleep. When told that "Grandmother went to heaven and became an angel," one five-year-old boy prayed that the rest of the family would die and become angels, too.

When a child is given the facts simply and honestly, accompanied by an affectionate hug and a loving look, that child feels reassured. This approach is effective when the parents themselves have accepted the realities of life and death. In all matters of importance, attitudes speak louder than words.

Growing up isn't easy. It is filled with disturbing thoughts and feelings, such as doubt, guilt, and especially anxiety. Children are afraid of being abandoned, are troubled by parental conflict, and confused and worried about death and dying. Parents cannot eliminate all of their children's anxiety, but they can help them cope better when they express understanding of their children's concern and prepare them for disturbing and fearful events.

CHAPTER 9

Sex and Human Values:

Sensitive Handling of an Important Subject

Many parents don't want to know about their children's sexual behavior, and adolescents are not eager to share their intimate life with their parents, especially if they think their parents would disapprove. As one mother in a parenting group related, "When I was young, I wanted to be independent of my parents' moral judgment. I made love without guilt or remorse. But now I'm a mother of a teenage daughter. Intellectually, I can accept the idea that she will have sex, but I don't want to know about it. I don't want her to consult me or share with me."

In fact, parents can be so overwhelmed by the thought of their children as sexual beings, they can be oblivious to their children's sexual behaviors.

A team of researchers at the University of Minnesota Center for Adolescent Health and Development released a report in September of 2000 saying that half of the mothers of sexually active teenagers mistakenly believe that their children are still virgins. Dr. Robert Blum, director of the center, said that the study did not examine why so many mothers (not fathers, because too few of them responded) were unaware of their children's sexual activity.

Communication between parents and children is effective, especially among teenagers, only within the context of a *trusting and caring relationship*. Only when young people feel that they can easily approach their parents, who *will listen to their point of view, won't yell, criticize, or dismiss what they have to say*, will they discuss their concern about sex. Says thirteen-year-old Selma, "I can't ask my mother anything about sex. If I do, she starts wondering why I asked the questions: 'What do you want to know for?' she asks." Twelve-year-old Juliet reports, "My mother believes that ignorance assures innocence. She gets mad when I ask her anything about sex. She usually answers, 'You'll learn all you need to know when you get older.'"

There are parents, mostly of teenage boys, who are comfortable with, and even encourage, their sons' sexual relationships. In contrast, there are others who would prefer not to be informed of their children's sexual experiences because they don't know how to respond without either making their youngster feel guilty or sanctioning premarital sex.

The following incident illustrates how Charles' father, despite initial shock, avoided this dilemma. Charles, age seventeen, came home after completing his junior year at a boarding school.

CHARLES: I have the greatest girlfriend.

FATHER: Hm.

CHARLES: I really like her. I'm going to see her tomorrow.

FATHER: You have a date.

CHARLES: I met her last week in school. She dated Larry first, but I could see she liked me. I went to bed with her before I actually liked her. But now I know her and I like her a lot.

FATHER (*stunned by the outpouring of more information than he cared to hear*): Oh, Charles, you met a girl you really like. How exciting!

CHARLES: We were together all last week and now I really like her a lot. I can hardly wait to see her again.

FATHER: It sounds like your last week in school was a really happy one. I bet you've had many new experiences this year.

CHARLES: Yes, you wouldn't believe how much I've learned in my music courses. I sure don't feel like the same person. I guess going away to school matured me.

Instead of preaching and moralizing, which may have made his son feel guilty, or reluctant to confide in his father in the future, Charles' father concentrated on his son's delight in a newfound love, and in the process helped him see himself as a maturing person.

But some parents, especially religious ones, for whom premarital sex is a sin, think that making their children feel guilty for even innocent sexual interests is an effective way of *teaching values*.

Thirteen-year-old Samantha, who knew how her mother felt about anything sexual, sought permission to have a junior high-school graduation party that her friends would enjoy.

SAMANTHA: Can I have a graduation party?

MOTHER: If you wish.

SAMANTHA: Do you know what some kids do at parties? They play kissing games.

MOTHER: Oh.

SAMANTHA: You know it might happen at my party. Is it okay? I don't know if we will. If it's up to me, we won't, but we might. Do you approve?

MOTHER: I'll have to think about it.

SAMANTHA: Do you know that the Bible approves of sex?

MOTHER: For whom?

SAMANTHA: For husband and wives?

MOTHER: Of course, for married people.

SAMANTHA: What about the party. Do you approve?

MOTHER: What do you think?

SAMANTHA: I think you'll say no. Is that right?

MOTHER: That's right.

SAMANTHA: Tell me why? I just want to know the reason.

MOTHER: Well, I think boys and girls your age are too young. Kissing and loving are for married adults.

SAMANTHA (*groaning*): I knew you'd say something like that.

What an opportunity Samantha's mother missed to make her daughter feel comfortable with her budding sexual interest. She could have said to her inquisitive daughter, "I can see that you are interested in understanding romantic relationships, but I don't think this game is appropriate for someone your age. Let's think of something else you and your friends might enjoy." Instead she added more guilt to an already guilt-ridden girl.

Parents' Own Sensuality

Sex education starts with the parents' attitudes toward their own sensuality. Do they like the sights and smells and feel of their bodies, or do they think that there is something unpleasant about them? Do they delight in each other's naked presence, or do they close their eyes and clothe their bodies in shame? Do they have any special aversions to their own or the partner's sex, or do they appreciate it? Do they see each other as inconsiderate and exploitive, or as exciting initiators of shared pleasures?

Whatever the parents' unspoken feelings are, they will be conveyed to the children, even if their spoken words try to hide them. This is the reason why it is so difficult to tell parents precisely what to reply to a child's questions about sex. Their own bewilderment in this area must first be acknowledged and their worries and embarrassment modified.

Beginning of Sexual Feelings

From birth on, infants are equipped to feel body pleasures, and from birth on, sex attitudes are in the process of forming. As soon as they are physically able, they explore their bodies. They handle their limbs and delight in being touched, tickled, and cuddled; this early touching and stroking are part of their sex education. Through them they learn to receive love.

There was a time when mothers were warned against cuddling and playing with their babies, lest they be spoiled. Even then, this maxim did not make sense to parents because their own need and desire to hug, cuddle, and embrace their baby was much stronger than any rule. Now we know that a baby needs a great deal of tender touching and of cuddly care and that both parents need to fulfill that need. It creates a mutual happy experience, and a special bond between baby and parent. Mothers who breast-feed their infants have the added pleasure of a mutually satisfying experience.

When children discover that the mouth grants extra pleasure, anything they can move goes there: a thumb, a blanket, a toy. The sucking, chewing, and biting bring pleasant sensations even when applied to inedible objects. These mouth pleasures should not be stopped, only regulated; we must see to it that what goes into the mouth is hygienic. Some infants get all their oral pleasures in eating; others need supplemental sucking, which should be granted unstintingly. During the first year or so, the mouth is the main mirror by which the world is reflected to the child. Let it be a pleasant reflection.

Sex and Toilet Training

During the second year of life children become more focused on the pleasures of evacuation. For them there is nothing disgusting in the sight, smell, and touch of feces. While parents guide them into civilized elimination habits, special care must be taken not to infect them with disgust toward their body and its products. Harsh and hasty measures may make the children feel that their body and all of its functions are something to dread, rather than to enjoy.

Impatient training is self-defeating. The average child may be ready for daytime control between two and a half and three years of age. Nighttime control may come between the third and fourth birthdays. Accidents, of course, are expected and need to be acknowledged: "Oh, you didn't quite make it to the bathroom this time. You were too busy building a tower. Let me help you get cleaned up."

Lack of training is also self-defeating. When children are left completely to their own devices, they may continue wetting and soiling for a long time. It may be pleasurable to some children, but meantime they miss the satisfactions that come with real accomplishments. When the child is ready, he or she should be told clearly and kindly what is expected: "Now that you're not a baby anymore but a big boy, Mommy and Daddy want you to let us know when you need to go and we will put you on the potty."

Answering Questions

Sex education has two parts: *information* and *values*. Information can be given in school, church, or at home. But values are best learned at home. Children learn about sexual and loving relationships by observing their parents interact with each other. Seeing their parents kissing, hugging, or making sexual overtures answers many of their questions about sex and love. It also encourages them to be open with their own affectionate and loving feelings.

In sex education, parents must forgo the temptation to give too much too soon. While there is no reason why children's sex questions cannot be answered frankly, the answers need not be a course in obstetrics. They can be brief, phrased in a sentence or two, not in long paragraphs or chapters.

The right age to inform a child about sexual matters is when the child asks questions. When a two- or three-year-old boy points to his genitals and wonders, "What is it?" it's the right moment to tell him, "It's your penis." Although children may refer to the penis as a peepee or weenie, the adult should call it by its rightful name.

When a child wonders where a baby comes from, we shall not tell her that it comes from the hospital or the stork. We tell her, "It grows inside a special place in a mother's body." Depending on further questions, it may or may not be necessary at this time to identify the place as the uterus.

In general, from early childhood on, children should learn the names and functions of their organs and the anatomical differences between the sexes. The explanations should not involve plants and animals.

Two questions puzzle almost all preschool children: How is a baby conceived? And how does it get born? It is advisable to hear the child's version before giving our own. Her answers usually involve food and elimination. One bright child explained, "Good babies start from good food. They grow in Mommy's stomach and pop out from her belly button. Bad babies start from bad food. They come out from the B.M. place."

Our explanation should be factual, but it does not need to give a full account of sexual intercourse: "When a father and a mother want to have a baby, a fluid called semen with many tiny sperm cells from the father's body joins an egg cell in the mother's body. The joining of the two cells starts the baby growing. When the baby is big enough, it comes out through the mother's vagina." Sometimes a child demands to be shown the place he came from. It is best not to allow such invasion of privacy.

Instead, we can draw a human figure, use a doll for demonstration, or make use of a book with illustrations.

Our answers may satisfy the child for a short while only. He may come back with the same, or with additional, questions. The child's next question may be the one parents dread: "How does the father's sperm cell get into the mother's egg cell?" Again, *we shall first ask the child for his version of the event*. We shall probably hear theories of "seed planting" (Daddy plants a seed into Mommy), of "seed eating" (Daddy tells Mommy to swallow a fruit pit), of pollination (the wind makes the seeds fly into the mother), of operation (the doctor plants a seed in the mother through surgery).

The child's question can then be answered briefly: "The semen comes out from the father's penis. It fits into the mother's vagina." This may be a good time to emphasize that semen is different from urine: "Urine is a body waste. Semen is a fluid that carries sperm cells."

The next question that may pop up is "When do you and Daddy make babies?" This is not as snoopy a question as it sounds. And a simple answer will suffice: "Mothers and fathers choose a time when they are comfortable and alone. They love each other and want to have a baby to love." It may also be necessary to add that the getting together or mating is a personal and private event.

Some boys wish that fathers, too, were able to have babies. They ask, "Why doesn't the mother egg go into the father?" The explanation is offered that a woman's body has a place—the uterus—in which a baby can grow. A man's body does not. It is not unusual for a child to ask, "Why?" A simple answer: "Because men's and women's bodies are built differently." It is desirable to assure the boys that babies also need a father to love them and protect them.

At the end of the day, parents have to remember that although talking about sex with their children can, more often than not, be very awkward, keeping a sense of humor will help them get through even the most tense situations. One mother recounted this amusing story: "My two-and-a-half-year-old son Paul asked me whether I had a penis. When I said no, he asked what I had there instead. I answered, 'Mommies have a special place.' Paul asked, 'What is it called?' I told him the word, thinking he was too young to understand all this. One day several weeks later, I was pushing Paul in his stroller into a crowded elevator in our building. A loud-voiced older woman began to interrogate him: 'What's your name? Are you having a nice holiday? Can you say hi?' Silence. I leaned over and whispered in Paul's ear, 'Say hi.' 'Hi!' he screamed at the top of his lungs. The woman shrieked, 'Oh, at least he can say hi!' Paul fixed her with a stare and said clearly, 'I can say vagina, too.' The elevator rocked with laughter and I could barely keep my composure. When we got inside our apartment he said, 'That's the biggest word I know.'"

The Naked Body

In childhood, the sight of naked Mom or Dad may stimulate sexual excitement in children. Does it mean that we must go back to Victorian prudery? Not at all. But it does mean that we need privacy, not only for our own peace but also for the sake of the children's development. We may tolerate children's occasional intrusions and stares when we are showering and dressing, but we should not encourage such behavior. We should especially be careful not to lead children to believe that we want them to explore us.

We recognize that children are curious about the human body. They have had a chance to observe the differences between little boys and girls, and they have also had occasional glimpses at us. And they would like to see more of us. It is best to recognize openly their curiosity, but insist on reasonable privacy. "You may want to see how I look, but when I take a bath I like to be alone. We can look at some pictures that will answer your questions." This approach does not attack or block the child's curiosity; it only diverts it into more socially acceptable channels. Curiosity can be expressed by words rather than by looking and touching.

Masturbation

Childhood masturbation is pleasurable and may bring comfort to children, but it causes conflicts to many parents. Children may find in it self-love when lonely, self-employment when bored, and self-consolation when rejected. To parents, it brings vague anxiety and concern. Most parents have heard, read, and even experienced masturbation as harmless. They know that it does not cause insanity, sterility, impotence, or any of a dozen other plagues. But when they come across their children playing with their sex organs, they get upset and try to stop them. Intellectually, parents recognize that masturbation may be a phase in the development of normal sexuality or it may continue into adulthood. Still, it is hard for some parents to accept that their child is masturbating.

However, masturbation is a natural part of a child's sexual experimentation. Parents who have problems with their child engaging in this activity in public places—at the dinner table or in the car—should remind the child that those pleasurable activities should be kept private. It is important not to overreact or shame the child—only a small direct comment is needed—"That kind of touching feels nice, but it is a private act for your room."

Forbidden Games

Infants like to investigate their bodies, and children to explore each other. Many of us remember as small children saying to a friend of the opposite sex, making sure our parents couldn't see us, "I'll show you mine if you show me yours." This thirst for knowledge is not easily quenched. The difference in anatomy baffles children who need to find out that being different does not mean there is anything wrong with them. Even when the facts are explained and the feelings understood, children may go on with mutual exploration. They invent games, such as playing doctor or house. They may also negotiate and arrange peeping games. Even sexually enlightened parents find it difficult to cope unemotionally with such situations. They may refrain from spanking or shaming the child, but they are not sure how to set a positive limit on such activities. In our day and age some parents even wonder if they should interfere in such intimate affairs, for fear of harming their offspring's future sex life.

When a two- or three-year-old girl watches how a little boy urinates, it is considered par for the course in anatomy. In nursery school, where children share the same toilets, curiosity can be satisfied by direct observation. However, by the first grade, a child is presumed to have seen enough. When a parent finds a boy and a girl with pants down and dress up, she should not ask them, "What are you doing?" (It may be too embarrassing if the child replies with the whole truth.) The children *should not be shamed or berated* with comments such as, "What is the matter with you? You should be ashamed of yourselves! Jimmy, I want you to go home right now. And with you, Melissa, I will deal later." On the other hand, they should not be provided with an easy excuse or a false alibi, such as "Don't you think it is too cold to walk around naked?" The children should be told, "Jimmy, Melissa, both of you need to get dressed now and find something else to play with." Our calm, unalarming attitude makes it possible to limit sexual experimentation without harming the child's interest in sex and love.

Dirty Words

No parent really wants their children to be naive about dirty words used by their peers. These words are so vigorous, expressive, and forbidden that they make the children feel big and important. When children use a string of dirty words in a secret council, they feel as though they have just composed their declaration of independence.

Four-letter words have a place that must be delineated and defined for the child. Parents should express their feelings on the subject frankly: The mother can say, "I don't like them at all, but I know children and even some adults use them. I prefer not to hear them. Spare them for your friends." Again, we recognize and *respect the children's wishes and feelings, but set limits and redirect their actions.*

Homosexuality

Some parents get upset as they watch their preadolescent children form close, even passionate relationships with friends of the same sex. They are worried about their child's sexual orientation mostly because they are concerned about the challenges their child may face when they openly acknowledge their homosexuality. In preadolescence, boys flock together and girls team up in intimate friendships. Much of the time they talk about sex. They compare notes and tell and retell what each has discovered. This same-sex friendship is a necessary prelude to the development of heterosexual love.

There are children who experiment with friends of the same sex. But we now know that unless they are so inclined, they will choose heterosexual mates. The researchers E. O. Laumann, J. H. Gagnon, R. T. Michael, and S. Michaels of the Kinsey Institute for Sex Research at Indiana University reported in 1994 that even though many people admitted having had some homosexual experiences, only about 4 percent of men and 2 percent of women consider themselves homosexual. *Confusion about sexual orientation is not unusual during adolescence.*

Lucky are the children whose parents are open and accepting, thus allowing them to share their concerns about their sexual feelings. What can experts tell parents? Years ago homosexual adolescents were sent for psychological treatment, but even Freud was not optimistic about changing a person's sexual orientation. Today we know that to a large extent homosexuality is biologically influenced and, thus, there is more acceptance and less of an attempt to change a person's sexual orientation.

When talking to their children about homosexuality,

parents should not pass judgment or make moral implications. Also, don't avoid discussing what exactly goes on when a man loves a man, not a woman. Be honest and give your children the best information you have on the subject. Your kids will thank you for trusting them with the truth instead of running for the hills when they ask, "Why does Rebecca have two mommies?"

Sex Education

In life, literature, television, and in the movies sexual taboos have been tumbling. The temper of our time is candor and feedom. Sex is no longer a forbidden subject. It is taught in school and discussed at home. Even in church, morality is reevaluated in light of reality. And in reality sex has always been a popular subject.

Teenagers are eager to learn all they can about sex. They are bothered and perplexed and want realistic and personal answers. When offered an opportunity to discuss sex seriously, teenagers talk freely and sensibly. They look for standards and meaning. They want to come to terms with their sexuality and to integrate it into their total personality.

Sharing Sexual Experiences

Jason, age fifteen, talked to his father about sex and love. He said, "I have discovered the real difference between boys and girls. Girls promise sex to get love and boys promise love to get sex. Love them and leave them is my philosophy."

FATHER: What happens to the girl after you love her and leave her?

JASON: It's not my business. I try not to think about it.

FATHER: Well, think about it. If you lure a girl into sex by promising love, her feelings become your business.

Jason's father affirmed his *values* that *honesty and responsibility pertain to all human relations. All situations, simple or complex, social or sexual, require individual integrity.*

Sixteen-year-old Natalie says, "My parents and I live by the grace of an unspoken code: 'No deep questions, no real answers.' They really don't want to know what goes on. And I can't tell them. I am, so to speak, a good girl."

"My father always blows his horn about being frank and truthful," is fifteen-year-old Joshua's complaint. "But his honesty stops where sex begins. This is one area where my candor is not welcome."

Parents need to encourage their teenagers to be honest with their feelings about sex: not to say "yes" when they want to say "no"; to listen to their needs, to respect their comfort; not to be too eager to please or to be part of a clique; not to have sex just to feel more grown-up than they are, and not to confuse a sexual relationship with a loving one.

Many parents are confused about their role in their adolescent's sexual life. Sally's mother consulted a psychologist when her seventeen-year-old daughter asked her to get her a supply of birth control pills: "I know my daughter. She's going to fall in love and want to make love. With pills she will, at least, be safe. But I'm uncomfortable making it easy for her to have sex."

"Teenagers who ask their parents for contraceptive pills indicate by their very request that they're not ready for adulthood," replied the psychologist. "By providing their adolescents with these pills, their parents deny them a vital experience: *to make decisions and accept the consequences.* An adult does not shift responsibility to her parents. She shoulders her own responsibility."

When Sally's mother came home, she informed her daughter, "Honey, if you think you're ready to have sex, then you are also ready to consult with your doctor about contraceptive pills. If I get you the pills, then I am, and you are not, involved in, and assuming responsibility for, your behavior."

Mature Love

"Only love justifies sex," said sixteen-year-old Betty. "So I'm always in love." This cynical approach has a social history. Betty probably feels guilty and the only way she can justify her sexual behavior is to fall in love. Love, real or imagined, expiates her guilt. But love is not just feeling and passion. Love is a system of attitudes and a series of acts that enhance life for both the lover and the beloved. Romantic love is often blind. It acknowledges the strength but does not see the weakness in the beloved. In contrast, *mature love* accepts the strength without rejecting the weakness. In mature love neither boy nor girl tries to exploit or possess the other. Each belongs to himself and herself. Such love gives freedom to unfold and to become one's best self. *Love and sex are not the same, but the lucky people are able to combine them.*

CHAPTER 10

Summing Up:

Lessons to Guide Your Parenting

What is the goal of parenting? It's to help a child grow up to be a decent human being, a mensch, a person with *compassion, commitment, and caring.* How does one go about humanizing a child? Only by using humane methods, by recognizing that the process is the method, that ends do not justify the means, and that in our attempt to be effective in getting children to behave, we do not damage them emotionally.

Children learn what they experience. They are like wet cement. Any word that falls on them makes an impact. It's therefore important that parents learn to talk to children in a way that is not enraging, doesn't inflict hurt, doesn't diminish their children's self-confidence, or cause them to lose faith in their competence and self-worth.

Parents set the tone of the home. Their response to every problem determines whether it will be escalated or de-escalated. Thus, parents need to discard a language of rejection and learn a language of acceptance. They even know the words. They heard their own parents use them with guests and strangers. *It's a language that is protective of feelings, not critical of behavior.*

A college student, dressed in jeans, was crossing the street when a cab driver almost hit him. Infuriated, the cabbie started to berate him: "Why don't you watch where you're going, you bum! You wanna get killed? Maybe you need your mother to hold your hand!"

The young man raised himself to his full height and calmly asked, "Is this the way you talk to a doctor?" The driver became contrite and apologized.

When parents talk to their children as if they were doctors, they neither provoke nor enrage them.

Thomas Mann, Nobel laureate in literature, said, "Speech is civilization itself." Yet words can brutalize as well as civilize, injure as well as heal. Parents need a language of compassion, a language that lingers lovingly. They need words that convey feelings, responses that change moods, statements that encourage goodwill, answers that bring insight, replies that radiate respect. The world talks to the mind. Parents speak more intimately, they speak to the heart, when they adopt a language of caring, which is sensitive to children's needs and feelings. It not only helps children develop a positive image of themselves that is confident and secure but also teaches them to treat their parents with respect and consideration.

However, it's not easy to substitute a language of caring for our usual way of talking. For example, Mr. Bloom had been attending a guidance group conducted for parents who wanted to learn a more effective yet caring way of communicating with children. After several meetings we had the following exchange:

MR. B: It seems that everything I have been saying to my children is wrong. Yet I find it very difficult to change my disciplinarian ways.

DR. G: It's not easy to change one's attitude and learn new skills.

MR. B: Not only that but if you're right, I've been treating my children without respect or dignity. No wonder they don't respect me or listen to me.

DR. G: You mean you're blaming yourself for not having known better?

MR. B: I guess you're right. As long as I blame myself, I'll also blame my children, instead of changing the way I talk to them. Okay, now I know what I have to do. I have to stop blaming and try to see if this language of caring you're advocating really works.

The rewards are great when parents make the effort to respond with care to their children, who hear the difference and learn to talk to their parents the same way.

Mr. Brown took his daughter, Debbie, age nine, to work with him the day his office was being painted. He reported the following conversation.

MR. B: I can't stand the smell of paint and all this dust. Everything is so disorganized.

DEBBIE: It must be awful for you to have to work like this. It's such a mess.

MR. B: Yes, it is.

DEBBIE: How did you like what I said to you?

MR. B: I liked it. I said to myself, "Debbie understands how I feel."

DEBBIE: I've been noticing that's the way you've been talking to me lately.

But parents need to be warned not to expect their children always to appreciate their new way of communicating, using a language that is caring. At times, children will insist that instead of acknowledging their feelings, a parent solve their problems, as this mother related.

One day, her eleven-year-old son, Noah, was complaining about his seven-year-old brother, Ron.

NOAH: I'm sick and tired of Ron's lying, cheating, and bothering me.

MOTHER: It must be very annoying. You come home after a long day at school and you are greeted by a younger brother who makes your life miserable.

NOAH: There you go again. I know how I feel. I don't need you to tell me.

MOTHER (*calmly, not defensively*): When someone tells me how I feel, I feel understood.

NOAH (*even angrier*): But I know you understand me. I think you take your classes with Dr. Ginott too seriously. I don't like the change in you.

MOTHER: How can I be of help?

NOAH: I want you to yell at Ron more.

MOTHER: But I'm learning that yelling doesn't solve anything.

NOAH: I need you to solve my problem with Ron.

MOTHER: I used to try to do that, but I don't anymore. That is the change you don't like. I have learned to have faith in your ability to solve your own problems.

NOAH: What about Ron's lying? I can't stand it.

MOTHER: Just last night your father told me that he was having a problem with Ron's lying and that his son, Noah, calmed him down by reminding him that it was just a stage. Can you imagine an eleven-year-old boy helping his father respond calmly to a child's misbehavior?

NOAH: I guess I did help him. Maybe I can help myself, too.

It takes skill not to revert to the old way of responding to children when attacked. This mother did not let Noah decide her mood nor lessen her resolve to continue to practice what she had learned. Because she felt caring and comfortable when she acknowledged her son's predicament, she did not try to justify herself or give in to his demand to solve his problem. Instead, she helped him develop faith in his ability to solve his own problems and thus helped him to grow up.

Discipline: Permissive of Feelings but Strict with Behavior

Parents want to know if the methods advocated in this book are strict or permissive regarding how they relate to discipline. They are *strict* when dealing with children's *misbehavior.* But *all feelings, wishes, desires, and fantasies are permissible,* be they positive, negative, or ambivalent. Like all of us, children cannot help how they feel. At some time they feel greed, lust, guilt, anger, fear, sadness, delight, and disgust. While they cannot choose their emotions, they are responsible for how and when they express them.

Unacceptable behavior is not tolerated. It's frustrating to try to *force* children into changing unacceptable behavior. Yet many parents still ask themselves ineffective questions: How to *make* Mark do chores? How to *force* Freddy to buckle down on schoolwork? How to *get* Grace to clean her room? How to *convince* Connie not to stay out later than her curfew? How to *impose* on Ivan some semblance of a routine?

Parents need to become convinced of the futility of nagging and pushing. Coercive tactics only breed resentment and resistance. External pressure only invites defiance. Instead of trying to impose their will on children, parents are more likely to influence them when they see their children's points of view and involve them in solving a problem.

An example: "Freddy, your teacher has informed us that you've not been doing your homework. Could you tell us what seems to be the problem? Is there any way we can help?"

Whatever eleven-year-old Freddy answers, the parents have started a dialogue that will get at the source of the problem and thus help Freddy assume responsibility for his homework.

Children need a clear definition of what is acceptable and what is unacceptable behavior. It's difficult for them not to act out their impulses and desires without parental help. When they know the clear limits of permissive behavior, they feel more secure.

It's *easier* for parents to make rules and state restrictions, *to set limits than to enforce them.* Parents are tempted to be flexible when children challenge rules. Parents want their children to be happy. When parents refuse to allow their children to break rules, the children may make the parents feel unloved and guilty.

"No more TV tonight," a father stated when his ten-year-old son's program finished. Steven became furious and yelled, "You're so mean! If you loved me, you would let me watch my favorite program, which is coming up next." The father was tempted to give in. It was not easy for him to refuse such pleas. But he decided not to set a precedent. He enforced the limit he set.

Because many rules are difficult to enforce, parents may want to prioritize their rules and try to have as few as possible.

It's Possible to Be Caring and Effective with Children

The following application of the principles of empathic communication can help parents be caring and effective in relating to their children.

1. *The beginning of wisdom is listening.* Listening that is empathic enables parents to hear the feelings that the words try to convey, to hear what children are feeling and experiencing, to hear their point of view and thus understand the essence of their communication.

Parents need an open mind and an open heart, which will help them to *listen to all kinds of truths,* be they pleasant or unpleasant. But many parents are afraid of listening because they may not like what they hear. Unless parents create a climate of trust that encourages their children to share even their disturbing feelings, opinions, complaints, and ideas, children will not be truthful. They will only tell their parents what they want to hear.

How can parents create a climate of trust? By the way they respond to *unpleasant truths*. The following parental comments are *not* helpful:

> *"What a crazy idea"* (dismissing)
> *"You know you don't hate me"* (denying)
> *"You're always going off half-cocked"* (criticizing)
> *"What makes you think you're so great?"* (humiliating)
> *"I don't want to hear another word about it!"* (getting angry)

Instead, *acknowledge*: "Oh, I see. I appreciate your sharing your strong feelings with me. So, that's your considered opinion. Thank you for bringing it to my attention." *Acknowledging is not agreeing.* It's only a respectful way of opening a dialogue, by taking children's statements seriously.

2. *Do not deny your child's perceptions, do not dispute his feelings, do not disown his wishes, do not deride his taste, do not denigrate his opinions, do not derogate his character, do not argue with his or her experience. Instead, acknowledge.*

At a swimming pool, eight-year-old Robert refused to jump in: "The water is too cold," he cried, "and I don't feel so well." His father responded, "The water's fine. It's you who are all wet. The pool is heated, but you have cold feet. You are scared like a rabbit and cry like a baby. You have a strong voice but a weak character."

His father's words *denied the child's perception, argued with his experience, disputed his feelings, and derogated his character.*

A helpful response that acknowledges the child's feelings would have been, "You don't feel well and the water seems cold. You wish you didn't have to jump in the pool today." Such a response tends to diminish resistance. The child feels accepted and respected. His words are taken seriously and he is not blamed.

When Mary, age ten, complained to her mother, "The soup is too salty," her mother automatically denied her daughter's perception and answered, "No, it's not. I hardly put in any salt." Had the mother learned to *acknowledge* her daughter's perception, she would have answered, "Oh, it's too salty for *you!" Acknowledging does not mean agreeing.* It only expresses respect for the child's opinion and, in this case, taste buds.

3. *Instead of criticism, use guidance. State the problem and possible solution.* Do not say anything negative to the child about herself. A mother noticed that her daughter's library book was overdue. Upset, she lashed out, criticizing, "You're so irresponsible. You always procrastinate and forget. Why didn't you return the book to the library on time?" Using guidance, the mother would have stated the problem and given the solution: "The book needs to be returned to the library. It's overdue."

4. *When angry, describe what you see, what you feel, and what you expect, starting with the pronoun "I":* "I'm angry, I'm annoyed, I'm furious, I'm indignant, I'm aghast." Avoid attacking the child. When Billy's father saw his four-year-old son throw stones at his friend, he did not insult and shame his child with comments such

as, "Are you crazy? You could have crippled your friend. Is that what you want? You're a cruel child." Instead he said loudly, "I'm angry and dismayed. We don't throw stones at people. People are not for hurting."

5. *In praising,* when you want to tell your children what you appreciate about them or their effort, *describe the specific acts. Do not evaluate character traits.* Betty, age twelve, helped her mother rearrange the kitchen cabinets. Her mother avoided using adjectives, being evaluative: "You did a good job. You're a hard worker. You'll make a great homemaker." Instead she described what Betty had accomplished: "The dishes and glasses are all in order now. It'll be easy for me to find what I need. It was a lot of work, but you did it. Thank you." The mother's words of recognition allowed Betty to make her own inference: "My mother liked what I did. I'm a good worker."

6. *Learn to say "no" in a less hurtful way by granting in fantasy what you can't grant in reality.* Children have difficulty in distinguishing between a *need* and a *want.* As far as they're concerned, anything they ask for, they need: "Can I get a new bicycle? I really need it. Can I, please?" In a toy store: "I want this truck. Please buy it for me." How is a parent to reply? Preferably not with a curt "No! You know we can't afford it." It's less hurtful at least to acknowledge children's wishes by describing your understanding of their desire: "Oh, how I wish we could buy you a new bicycle. I know how much you would enjoy riding around town and to school. It would make life so much easier for you. Right now, our budget will not allow it. Let me talk to your father and see what we can do for Christmas." Or, "How I wish I had the money to buy it for you," rather than, "Everything you see you want. No, you can't have it, so stop asking."

Elizabeth, age seventeen, asked her mom, "I need your diamond earrings to wear to the prom. Can I have them?" Angered, her mother replied, "Absolutely not! You know I don't let anyone wear my diamond earrings. What if you lose them?" A less hurtful response would have been to acknowledge the child's wish: "How I wish I had an extra pair of diamond earrings to give you. Is there anything else in my jewelry box you would like?"

It's difficult for parents to deny their children's requests. They would like to fulfill their desires. They want to see them happy. Thus parents get frustrated and angry when demands are made that they can't satisfy and are harsh when they have to say "no." By acknowledging the wish and not getting angry, parents make it possible for children to express their feelings.

7. *Give children a choice and a voice in matters that affect their lives.* Children are dependent on their parents, and dependency breeds hostility. To reduce enmity, a parent provides children with opportunities to experience independence. The more autonomy, the less enmity; the more self-dependence, the less resentment of the parent.

Even a small child can be asked, "Would you like jam or butter on your toast?" Or told, "Bedtime is between seven and eight. You decide when you're tired enough to go to sleep." What difference does it make for a child to be given choices? She may say to herself, My parents take my wishes into account. I have something to say about my life. I'm a person. I matter.

I received the following letter in response to a newspaper column in which I discussed giving children choices:

In one of your columns you reminded us that even very small children need to be able to make some choices. And that is what I want especially to thank you for, and to say that holds equally true at the other end of life, when a person may again be as helpless as a small child.

I was with my eighty-year-old father while he was dying of cancer. Watching his depression at being so dependent brought back your words loud and clear. How awful not to have control over your life. I thought it might help lessen his frustration if he could make some valid choices. There were a surprising number of situations that he could and should have a say in, such as, Did he want me to help him into the bathroom (modesty does disappear at some point, but it should be for him to decide when)? Would he like me to talk to him or would he rather I sat quietly? Would he like lunch? Did he want his grandchildren to visit?

Some of them were simple things, but all of them were things in which I felt he should have a choice. I also feel that this helped establish a certain kind of rapport with him that I hate to think I might have missed. I hope, too, that I helped somewhat to ease not his pain, unfortunately, but the burden of dying.

Epilogue

The solutions offered in this book can lighten the task of parenthood only when applied appropriately. Children vary in their responses to demands. Some children are compliant; they easily accept change in routines and relationships. Others, more conservative, accept change only under protest and after prodding. Still others actively resist any "new deal" in their lives. A wise application of the approach advocated in this book will not ignore the basic grain of the child's temperament and personality.

Children flourish only when methods of child rearing are imbued with respect and sympathy. This approach can create *deeper sensitivity to feelings and greater responsiveness to needs* in the challenging relationship between parent and child.

A young couple lost their way in the maze of California

highways. "We are lost," they said to the police officer at the toll booth.

"Do you know where you are?" he inquired.

"Yes," answered the couple. "It says so on your booth."

"Do you know where you want to go?" continued the officer.

"Yes," replied the couple in unison.

"Then you are not lost," concluded the officer. "You only need clear directions."

Parents can also benefit from clear directions to help them get to where they want to go in bringing up their children. But in addition they also need luck and skill. One may ask, "With luck, why do they need skill?" So as not to spoil the luck.

How Children Can Be Helped

Even children who are not disturbed react with emotional upset to stressful situations or inner conflicts. They may have fears and nightmares, bite their nails, bait brothers and sisters, suffer from tics and tantrums, and act in many other disturbing ways. They are wanted children, reared by loving parents, from unbroken homes, who may benefit from child therapy.

Recent trauma.   Children exposed to a sudden catastrophe may develop post-traumatic stress disorder. A child may react with overwhelming anxiety and develop dramatic symptoms when witnessing a fire, a car accident, or a terrorist attack. The death of a beloved person can be especially devastating.

When terrorists, using planes as weapons, attacked the United States and destroyed the Twin Towers in downtown New York City on September 11, 2001, adults and children were severely traumatized. Many children lost a parent and some even both. The surviving, mourning parent or relative was left to cope with the bereaved and distraught children.

Viewing the fiery Twin Towers on television or from a safe distance was also traumatic for both children and adults, but the psychological impact was far worse for children who had a firsthand experience or a parent who escaped from the conflagration. According to a study reported in the *New York Times,* the closer the child was to the disaster area, the more traumatic was the response.

Small children who live through traumatic experiences seldom talk about it. Their fears and tensions come out in their play. Child psychotherapy provides an appropriate setting, suitable materials, and a sympathetic adult to help children in their hour of great need. The therapist enables them to relive, through play and words, the fearful events so that they may assimilate and master their panic and anxiety. They build houses out of blocks and drop bombs on them. Sirens scream, fires rage, and ambulances remove the injured and dead. For weeks they play out their feelings of shock and horror. Only after such symbolic reenactment of the events are children able to talk about their feelings and memories without fear and anxiety. Anxiety generated by a recent disaster is diminished when, in the presence of an understanding adult, the child is able to reenact with toys, and to tell in words, the fearful events and memories. With the help of many professional volunteers, New York City made psychological help available for those in need.

Fearful children. Like ham and eggs, little children and fears go together. Dogs seem to be the main fear of three-year-olds, darkness of four-year-olds. These fears decline with age, disappearing completely by the age of eight. Other fears reported by many children were of fire engines, sirens, earthquakes, kidnapping, fast driving, snakes, and high places. Since 9/11 the predominant fear is of terrorists. Some of the children showed slight apprehension, but did not withdraw from the situation if a parent was around. Others felt greater discomfort; they wanted the light on at night or showed tension when a fire engine passed or a burglary was mentioned.

Children with persistent and intense fears can benefit from professional help. The intensity of their reaction is the telling clue. They are paralyzed and incapacitated by their anxiety: The sky may fall down, lightning may strike the house, the whole family may be swept away by a hurricane. There is no end to their kaleidoscope of feared objects and people: loud noises, high places, new people, running water, dark corners, small insects, and large animals. They try to escape anxiety by avoiding places and activities that seem threatening to them. Thus they may stay away from water, avoid climbing a ladder, or refuse to stay in a dark room.

In group psychotherapy, fearful children are likely to engage in activities that will require them to deal with their fears. They may shoot noisy cap guns, use finger paints, cover themselves with mud, or turn out the lights. The group makes it impossible for fearful children to escape facing their problem. The therapist can then deal with the fearful reactions as they occur. Children are helped to play out and talk out their frantic fears and to lessen and master their vague anxiety.

Too-intense sibling rivalry. Children whose jealousy of their siblings pervades their whole personality and colors their whole life need psychological help. They abuse their brothers and sisters both physically and verbally. Experiencing their sibling as their parents' favorite, they seek exclusive attention and try in every possible way to become the favorite of a teacher, Scout leader, or camp counselor. Competitive, they have a compelling need to excel and do not handle defeat well. If the jealousy of such youngsters is not diminished in childhood, they may go through life treating people as though they were substitute siblings. They may also continue consciously to make life miserable for their brothers and sisters.

It is normal for children to be jealous of brothers and sisters, but unlike children who need help, their jealousy is not a pervasive pattern. They may feel that their siblings receive more love, and they may vie with them for affection. But when they receive love, they are readily reassured. They, too, may like competition and excelling, but they can also enjoy games for the fun of playing. Moreover, they can accept defeat without much pain or strain.

Too-intense interest in sex.   Some children evidence premature and persistent preoccupation with sexual matters. They dream, think, and talk sex. They masturbate habitually in private or in public, and try to engage in sexual explorations with other children, including brothers and sisters. They peek, and attempt to "catch" their parents in sexual relations. Sex is on their mind too much and too soon. These children need psychological help.

Most children show a natural interest in sexual matters. They may tease the opposite sex, giggle about boyfriends or girlfriends. They may also be pleasurably conscious of their sensuality; they may touch themselves and masturbate occasionally. However, sex activity remains only a part of their life.

Extremely modest children.   These are children who get panicky when they are observed undressed. They are painfully self-conscious about their bodies; they are uncomfortable in classes of physical education and are mortified during a medical examination. They can benefit by professional help.

Other children may also dislike undressing for a physical examination or the gym. They may fuss and protest, but they do not panic.

Extremely aggressive children.   Very hostile children need professional help. The meaning of the hostility must be thoroughly evaluated and understood. Since hostility may stem from a variety of sources, it is necessary to find the cause of aggression in each specific case, so that treatment may be fitted to the cause and the case.

Occasionally we meet children whose aggression does not diminish with expression and whose destructiveness is not accompanied by visible guilt. Some of these children are capable of extreme cruelty without apparent anxiety or repentance. They seem to lack capacity for sympathy, and show no concern for the welfare of others. Censure and criticism have little effect on them, as though they were indifferent to what others think of them. Not even penalties impel them to make amends. They fear adults, distrust their kindliness, and reject their favors. Establishing a relationship with such children is not a simple matter. Children with such a history benefit from treatment when the therapist is able to win their trust and to establish a relationship based on mutual respect.

It's not unusual for children occasionally to engage in aggressive and destructive behavior. Much of it is due to curiosity and high energy. Some of it is due to frustration and resentment. The aggressive behavior may occur at home but not outside of it, or vice versa, at school but not at home. Children may destroy their own toys, from curiosity or from anger, but they are more cautious with the property of others.

Habitual stealing. Persistent stealing is a serious problem. Some children engage in petty, and not so petty, pilfering whenever an opportunity presents itself. They may steal at home, school, camp, the supermarket, or from neighbors. Children with long histories of stealing can benefit from group psychotherapy. Some of these children, usually older, steal to buy drugs. For these children a drug rehabilitation center is indicated.

Children who steal only at home do not belong to this category. They may also be involved in occasional episodes of mild pilfering outside the home. They may take fruits and candy, or fail to return "borrowed" or "found" items. However, this mode of behavior usually lasts briefly. As they grow older, these children come to recognize property rights and to respect them.

The too-good-to-be-trues. Some children seem too good to be real. They are obedient, orderly, and neat. They worry about their mother's health, are concerned about their father's business, and are eager to take care of their little sister. Their whole life seems to be oriented toward pleasing their parents. They have little energy left for playing with children their own age.

In school and in the neighborhood, such children may continue with their goody-goody behavior. They will be meek and gentle and spend their time and energy in placating the teacher, whom they fear. They may bring her the proverbial apple or volunteer to clean up the board. Under the goody-goody mask, many a "bad-bad" impulse is hidden. The effort of transforming hostile impulses into angelic behavior, and the eternal vigilance required to maintain a facade, consume the life energy of these children. It is not unusual to read about a child who committed a serious crime, only to have neighbors report how obedient, quiet, and helpful the child was.

Group psychotherapy provides an effective setting to modify overgood behavior. The setting, which includes children who are more direct with their hostile impulses, encourages these goody-goody children to give up slavish compliance and to assume normal assertiveness. By observation and experience they learn that there is no need to be ingratiating and self-effacing. They slowly begin to allow their hostile impulses to gain some expression. They come to discover their own wants, know their own feelings, and establish their own identity.

Immature children.   Under this heading are included children who are wanted and loved as babies, but not as growing individuals who have ideas and needs of their own. These overprotected children are unprepared for the realities of life outside the family shelter. They have little opportunity to develop appreciation for the needs and feelings of others, and they find it difficult to tolerate frustration. Instead of exerting their own efforts, they want others to care for them.

Psychotherapy in carefully selected groups is of particular value to immature children. The group offers motivation and support for growing up, as well as a safe arena for the trying out of new patterns of behavior. In the group they learn what aspects of their behavior are socially unacceptable, and what behavior is expected. As a result, they make an effort to adjust to the standards of their peers. In the group they learn a variety of essential social techniques, such as sharing materials and activities and the attention of a friendly adult. They learn to compete and to cooperate, to fight and to settle fights, to bargain and to compromise. These techniques prepare such children to deal with their contemporaries on an equal footing.

Withdrawn children.   These children can be described as shy, submissive, inhibited, and meek. They have difficulty expressing ordinary feelings of affection and aggression, have few friends, and avoid social games and play. They are ill at ease in interpersonal situations, and they avoid meeting new people. They want others to make the first friendly overture and even then they may not respond in kind.

Withdrawn children find it difficult to relate to the teacher in school or to classmates in the yard. They are mortified when called upon to read aloud or to answer a question. They may respond with a "yes" or a "no" answer, or not at all. When they play, they choose a quiet and safe activity that does not demand social give-and-take. When social contact is forced on them, their anxiety may mount to the point of panic.

Withdrawn children can be helped in group psychotherapy. The friendly adult, the enchanting materials, and the selected group members make it difficult for them to stay within their shells. The setting accelerates emergence from isolation and encourages freedom in play and conversation with other children.

Tics and mannerisms.   Some children exhibit persistent mannerisms that are annoying to parents. They squint, sniff, grimace, twitch, pick noses, rub eyes, clear throats, hunch shoulders, bite nails, suck thumbs, crack knuckles, or tap feet. The contortions and mannerisms may be so obvious and grotesque that they compel attention. The fingers may be disfigured, the skin waterlogged, or the nails bitten down to the quick. And there is no escape from the discordant sounds of noses, throats, knuckles, and feet. These children need psychological consultation, as well as medical attention, to determine the appropriate treatment.

Sometimes children who are fatigued, sleepy, preoccupied, or under some emotional strain may also exhibit a variety of mannerisms and tics. However, these manifestations are not persistent and eventually disappear.

How Child Psychotherapists Deal with Their Own Children

As a parent and child psychologist, I was often asked whether my professional training and experience was helpful in bringing up my own children. Do psychotherapists make better parents than people without training? This question is seldom asked, though the answer is not obvious. A group of child psychologists and psychiatrists met to discuss this *touchy* subject.

DR. ADAMS: The public expects its mental-health experts to be better parents. If they personally cannot benefit from their professional experience and insight, what hope is there for lay parents?

DR. BRUCE: On the other hand, the same public, not without delight, tells funny jokes about the disturbed and disturbing children of psychologists and psychiatrists.

DR. CHAMBERS: The question is, Can professional competence be personalized? *Can psychological principles be translated into child-rearing practices?*

DR. DAVID: I have my doubts. I am understanding and tolerant with my child patients. But I easily lose my temper with my own children. I get angry, I yell, nag, and insult. Just like a parent.

DR. FIELD (*to Dr. David*): In a lecture, you once said, "What counts in parent-child relations is not a particular method but general attitudes." I know you have a marvelous general attitude toward your own children. So, how is it that in daily existence you make their lives difficult?

DR. DAVID: I can't be objective with my own children. I am spontaneous. I don't use any deliberate methods with them.

DR. ADAMS: What's wrong with applying to your own children methods *proved helpful with your young patients*?

DR. DAVID: It seems so manipulative, so contrived, so lacking in spontaneity.

DR. GREEN: The world is full of disturbed adults who as children were given the "spontaneous treatment" by their parents. *What was on their lungs was on their tongues.* And their tongues spewed invectives and insults.

DR. DAVID: You mean, you are against being "spontaneous" with your own children?

DR. GREEN: No, not at all. What I'm against is *impulsivity masquerading as spontaneity.* There is nothing wrong in parents examining their natural reactions to their children—to separate the chaff from the wheat, *to learn what helps and what hurts.*

DR. DAVID: Are you saying that some of our spontaneous reactions may be damaging our children? You may be right. Even under provocation, it would never occur to me to call a young patient abusive names. Yet I do it to my own son.

DR. IVY: Same here. When one of my child patients accidentally spilled red paint in the playroom, I knew exactly how to respond: "Oh. The paint spilled. We need a sponge. And here is some water for you." It was a spontaneous, automatic remark. It was not *contrived* but neither was it *accidental. It was the result of my therapeutic training.*

DR. BRUCE: Suppose your son accidentally spilled paint on the rug at home. What then?

DR. IVY: Don't ask! Of course it would depend on my mood, but I have been known to blame, and shame: "Look what you did. You are clumsy. How many times do I have to tell you to be careful?" I can see how protective I am of my little patients and how destructive I can sometimes be with my *own* child. In the heat of the moment, I don't think of applying my *trained spontaneity* to my own son.

DR. ADAMS: A great master once told his students, "Learn techniques and then forget them." This is the *veritas* of every virtuoso. It applies also to us.

DR. BRUCE: Just as a surgeon cannot operate on his own family, a psychiatrist cannot be a therapist to his own children. Isn't there a danger that you will become a therapist, not a parent, to your child?

DR. ADAMS: Not at all. I give my child patients the best I've learned. And that includes properly timed interpretations of unconscious processes. I would not think of diagnosing or interpreting for my own children, of playing psychologist. But *what is sensitive, compassionate, and humane changes very little from office to home.*

DR. FIELD: I also found my training in medicine and psychiatry relevant to my own life. When my son broke his arm, I didn't faint at the sight of his bone sticking out of his skin. I administered first aid: not only physical but also emotional. And thus helped him cope with his *pain* and also his *panic*.

DR. HILL: I wonder why we apply so little of our clinical know-how to bringing up our own children. I, for instance, deal with my son essentially the way my mother dealt with me. I sometimes even use her tone of voice. It is as though I were replaying a familiar tape.

DR. CHAMBERS: Are you looking for an unfamiliar tape? A new script? The sound of a different drummer?

DR. HILL: I don't like my parental tape. Without being aware, many parents unconsciously recite past scripts. But we are aware. We should be able to write our own script and make use of all that we learned as child therapists.

DR. BRUCE: Yet you sound like a typical parent.

DR. HILL: I do, and it bothers me. At home, when things go wrong, I don't know how to turn it off. Like other parents, I regress and regret, even after my professional training and many years of treating children.

DR. BRUCE: All parents are vulnerable. It's not easy to win with your own children. Heads, we lose. Tails, they win.

DR. ADAMS: Children present concrete problems which do not yield to glittering generalities about love, respect, acceptance, individual differences, and personal uniqueness. These concepts are too large. They are like a thousand-dollar bill—good currency but useless in meeting daily needs, such as buying a cup of coffee, taking a cab, or making a phone call. For daily life we need coins. For child rearing, we need psychological small change, *akin to* that used in child therapy.

DR. DAVID: But pray tell me, what is psychological small change?

DR. ADAMS: Specific ways of dealing effectively and humanely with the minute-to-minute happenings: the small irritations, the periodic conflicts, the sudden crises.

DR. DAVID: Tell us how you as a parent have benefited from you as a therapist.

DR. ADAMS: I can give you a list as long as a book. But I am afraid you'll think I have all the answers. Well, I don't. But I have learned to respond more humanely to the daily difficulties presented by my children. I'm empathic as I'm with my child patients. *I try to put myself in their shoes to understand how they feel.* I have learned how to express anger without insult. Even under provocation, I don't call my children abusive names. I don't offend their personality attributes and don't attack their character traits. Instead, just as in therapy, *I state what I see, what I feel, and what needs to be done.*

DR. DAVID: You mean you don't lose your temper with your children?

DR. ADAMS: On the contrary. Now I am not afraid of my anger. Because I know how to express it without doing damage. I am *authentic*: My words fit my feelings. I don't pretend to feel loving when I'm angry. I have also learned that the beginning of wisdom is silence, and that authority calls for brevity. So *I talk less and I listen more*. When things go wrong, *I don't teach lessons, I look for solutions*. I've learned to respond to my children's complaints without being defensive or counter-complaining. I often employ sympathetic grunts and brief comments.

DR. CHAMBERS: Such as?

DR. ADAMS: "Oh. I see. So that's what happened. So that's how you feel. So that's your considered opinion. I appreciate your sharing your views with me. Thank you for bringing them to my attention. Let me write down your suggestions to help me remember." I deliberately avoid embarrassing questions. I avoid cold logic in hot situations. *Since the world talks to the mind, I talk to the heart.*

DR. BRUCE: That's just common sense.

DR. GREEN: No, I think it takes *uncommon sense*. For instance, in child therapy I have learned that even some praise can be destructive. So I don't use it. Either in the playroom or at home. I avoid praise that puts children under obligation to live up to the impossible: You are *always* so wonderful, you are *always* so considerate. You are an angel. My praise is appreciative: It *describes* the child's efforts and accomplishments and my feelings about them. It does not evaluate, judge, compare, or condescend.

DR. CHAMBERS: Could you elucidate a little more?

DR. GREEN: I like your request. It makes it possible for me to clarify my views. I appreciate your interest. You see, Dr. Chambers, that was appreciative praise.

DR. CHAMBERS: How would you have praised me before your training in child therapy?

DR. GREEN: "You're great. You always come to my aid. You're doing a marvelous job in this group." Have you noticed that with appreciative praise I started with the pronoun "I"? With judgmental praise I started with the pronoun "You."

DR. CHAMBERS: I can do without such praise.

DR. GREEN: So can children. Also, I don't deny a child's perception. I don't disown her feelings. I don't argue with his experience. *I acknowledge perception, feelings, and experience.*

DR. IVY: Then we, too, need help in fulfilling our parental roles. We need to recognize that our daily responses to our children are not without consequence. They affect conduct and character for better or for worse. We already possess the knowledge. What we need is to transfer competence and translate skill. This metamorphosis will not occur automatically. *But as psychotherapists we have a head start.*

Additional Resources

Parents face many challenges in bringing up their children. This book has not dealt with all the issues that parents face. Here are some books that may be helpful.

Benson, Herbert, and Miriam Z. Klipper. *The Relaxation Response (Updated and Expanded)*. New York: William Morrow & Co., 2000.

Bray, James H., and John Kelly. *Stepfamilies: Love, Marriage, and Parenting in the First Decade*. New York: Broadway Books, 1999.

Brazelton, T. B., and S. I. Greenspan. *The Irreducible Needs of Children: What Every Child Must Have to Grow, Learn, and Flourish*. Cambridge, Mass.: Perseus, 2000.

Burns, David D. *Feeling Good: The New Mood Therapy*. New York: William Morrow & Co., 1999.

Carlson, Barbara Z., and William J. Doherty. *Putting Family First: Successful Strategies for Reclaiming Family Life in a Hurry-Up World*. New York: Henry Holt & Company, 2002.

Csikszentmihalyi, Mihaly. *Finding Flow: The Psychology of Engagement with Everyday Life*. New York: Basic Books, 1998.

Doherty, William J. *Take Back Your Kids: Confident Parenting in Turbulent Times*. Notre Dame, Ind.: Sorin Books, 2000.

——. *The Intentional Family: Simple Rituals to Strengthen Family Ties*. New York: William Morrow & Co., 1999.

Eckler, James D. *Step-by Step-Parenting: A Guide to Successful Living with a Blended Family*. Des Moines, Iowa: F & W Publications, 1993.

Eisenberg, Arlene, Sandee Hathaway, and Heidi Murkoff. *What to Expect When You're Expecting*. New York: Workman Publishing Company, 2002.

——. *What to Expect the First Year*. New York: Workman Publishing Company, 1996.

——. *What to Expect in the Toddler Years*. New York: Workman Publishing Company, 1996.

Emberley, Michael, and Robie H. Harris. *It's So Amazing!: A Book About Eggs, Sperm, Birth, Babies, and Families*. Cambridge, Mass.: Candlewick Press, 1999.

——. *It's Perfectly Normal: Changing Bodies, Growing Up, Sex, and Sexual Health*. Cambridge, Mass.: Candlewick Press, 1996.

Faber, Adele, Elaine Mazlish, and Kimberly Ann Coe (illustrator). *How to Talk So Kids Will Listen and Listen So Kids Will Talk*. New York: William Morrow & Co., 1999.

——. *Siblings Without Rivalry: How to Help Your Children Live Together So You Can Live Too*. New York: William Morrow & Co., 1998.

Forehand, Rex L., and Nicholas James Long. *Parenting the Strong-Willed Child, Revised and Updated Edition: The Clinically Proven Five-Week Program for Parents of Two- to Six-Year-Olds*. New York: McGraw-Hill/Contemporary, 2002.

Ginott, Haim G. *Group Psychotherapy with Children*. New York: McGraw Hill, 1961.

Goldenthal, Peter. *Beyond Sibling Rivalry: How to Help Your Children Become Cooperative, Caring, and Compassionate*. New York: Henry Holt & Company, 2000.

Gottman, John M., with Joan DeClaire. *Raising an Emotionally Intelligent Child*. New York: Simon & Schuster, 1998.

Greenspan, Stanley I., and Jacqueline Salmon. *The Four-Thirds Solution*. Cambridge, Mass.: Perseus, 2001.

Kohn, Alfie. *Punished by Rewards: The Trouble with Gold Stars, Incentive Plans, A's, Praise, and Other Bribes*. Boston: Houghton Mifflin Company, 1999.

Nilsson, Lennart. *A Child Is Born*. New York: Bantam Doubleday Dell, 1990.

———, with Lena Katarina Swanberg. *How Was I Born?* New York: Dell, 1996.

Norcross, John C., John Santrock, Robert Sommer, Thomas Smith, Edward Zuckerman, and Linda Campbell. *The Authoritative Guide to Self-Help Resources in Mental Health*. New York: Guilford Publications, Inc., 2000.

Sandholtz, Kurt, Brooklyn Derr, Dawn Carlson, and Kathy Buckner. *Beyond Juggling: Rebalancing Your Busy Life*. San Francisco: Berrett-Koehler Publishers, 2002.

Santrock, John H., Ann M. Minnett, and Barbara D. Campbell. *The Authoritative Guide to Self-Help Books*. New York: Guilford Press, 1994.

Seligman, Martin E. *Authentic Happiness: Using the New Positive Psychology to Realize Your Potential for Lasting Fulfillment*. New York: The Free Press, 2002.

———. *Learned Optimism*. New York: Simon & Schuster, 1998.

———, with Jane Gillham, Karen Reivich, and Lisa Jaycox. *The Optimistic Child: A Proven Program to Safeguard Children Against Depression and Build Lifelong Resilience*. New York: HarperCollins, 1996.

———. *What You Can Change and What You Can't: The Complete Guide to Successful Self-Improvement*. New York: Ballantine Books, 1995.

Spock, Benjamin, Stephen Parker, and Sharon Scotland (illustrator). *Dr. Spock's Baby and Child Care, 7th Edition*. New York: Pocket Books, 1998.

Visher, Emily, and John Visher. *How to Win as a Stepfamily*. Levittown, Penn.: Brunner/Mazel, 1991.

Williams, Redford, and Virginia Williams. *Anger Kills: 17 Strategies for Controlling the Hostility That Can Harm Your Health.* New York: HarperCollins, 1998.

Worthington, Everett L. *Five Steps to Forgiveness.* New York: Crown Publishers, 2001.

In addition to the print resources listed above there are additional books and Web sites that may be useful. Some resources are far better than others. *The Authoritative Guide to Self-Help Resources* by John W. Santrock, et al., can help parents discern which books are most promising. It also lists some recommended Web resources.

There are many Web sites affiliated with universities or cooperative extension services that provide information that is solidly founded in respected research. For example, many excellent resources can be found at the Children, Youth and Families Education and Research Network (www.cyfernet.org). Such sites provide sensible information that is not influenced by sponsorship. By searching for keywords within such a site, you are likely to find many useful and timely resources.

Index

About the Authors

Dr. Alice Ginott is a noted psychologist, psychotherapist, author, and lecturer. Verbal communication is the focus of her skills. As she states: "We are unaware that words are like knives, that we need to be skilled in the use of words. Unlike a surgeon who is careful where he cuts, we use words randomly. We make many incisions until we hit  the right spot, heedless of the open wounds we leave behind. We perform daily emotional operations but we do it without training. Even people who love each other and their children lack a language that conveys that love, that mirrors their delight, that makes the one they love feel loved, respected, and appreciated." The purpose of her lectures, workshops, and guidance groups with couples, parents, and teachers is to help them enter the world of another in a compassionate and caring way.

Dr. Ginott's ideas of communicating with parents and teachers were disseminated in the King Features internationally syndicated column "Between Us." She reflects the enthusiasm, warmth, and humor found in her many articles, such as "How to Drive Your Child Sane" and "How to Help Children Mourn," which strive to revolutionize the way we talk to one another.

Dr. Ginott received her B.A. from Indiana University and her M.A. and Ph.D. from the Graduate Faculty of the New School University in New York. As a former assistant professor of psychology at Hunter and Queens colleges in New York, and a visiting scholar at Chatham College in Pittsburgh, she enjoys sharing her ideas with students. She was a member of the 1970 White House Conference on Children and was invited by the American University in Cairo, Egypt, to be the keynote speaker at a symposium for the International Year of the Child, in which Ms. Jihan el Sadat also participated. She has lectured widely in the United States, Brazil, Africa, Canada, Europe, India, Hong Kong, and Israel. She is also the recipient of the Eleanor Roosevelt Humanities award.

Dr. Ginott was born in the former Czechoslovakia, is the mother of two daughters—a physician and a lawyer—and has two grandchildren.

Dr. H. Wallace Goddard serves as an extension family life specialist for the University of Arkansas Cooperative Extension Service. In his work he develops programs on parenting, marriage, youth development, and family relations. He is also involved in writing books and Web articles, producing television programs, and developing national extension programs.

Dr. Goddard grew up in the mountains outside Salt Lake City, Utah. He got degrees at Brigham Young University in physics, math, and education before teaching high school in subjects ranging from general science to film-making, from folklore to gifted and talented, from media to literature.

After teaching school for a dozen years, he returned to school, this time Utah State University, for a Ph.D. in family and human development. His dissertation research created and tested a new parenting program that applied discoveries in attribution research to parenting. His research established the merits of helping parents interpret their children in the most favorable light.

Dr. Goddard served as an extension specialist at Auburn University in Alabama for six years. During that time he studied teen behavior (he surveyed 14,000 teens!), developed a widely used parenting program (Principles of Parenting), participated with a national team to develop a model of parent education (The National Extension Parent Education Model), and created a respected youth development program (The Great Self Mystery).

He took leave from Auburn University to help Stephen Covey write *The 7 Habits of Highly Effective Families* and to develop application activities for improving family life. He also taught courses for Utah State University.

Dr. Goddard came to Arkansas in order to work again as an extension specialist, a work that he loves. He has worked with colleagues to develop a wealth of family resources that are posted on the University of Arkansas Extension Web site (www.arfamilies.org). He also provides training to county extension agents, speaks to public groups, and is working with AETN on a series of television programs entitled *Guiding Children Successfully*. In addition to writing for popular Web sites, he is also working on a textbook on family-life education.

He and his wife, Nancy, have three adult children, and have cared for twenty foster children over the years. He travels extensively as a presenter and consultant and lives in Little Rock, Arkansas.